A MODERN MARTYR

A Modern Martyr

ADAPTED BY EDWARD A. MCGURKIN

FROM THE BOOK OF THE SAME TITLE

BY

Most Reverend

JAMES ANTHONY WALSH

*Titular Bishop of Siene, Cofounder
and First Superior General of
Maryknoll*

MCMULLEN BOOKS, INC.
NEW YORK

B
T

IMPRIMATUR: ✠ John Cardinal Farley
Archbishop of New York

DEDICATION

This book is dedicated to the Catholic youth of America in the hope and belief that among them many will be found to follow Christ the whole way into the wilderness for the souls that He has died to save.

"The world martyrs the Church, and the Church subdues the world. The words of Our Divine Lord are always verified, 'I come not to send peace upon earth, but a sword.' The age of martyrs, as of miracles, never ceases. Martyrdom is a perpetual note upon the Mystical Body, which has the Stigmata of Jesus ever fresh upon it."

—CARDINAL WISEMAN

Contents

Contents

A MODERN MARTYR

CHAPTER ONE

The Boy from Golden Valley

". . . . What a boy you were,
With your back-tilted hat and careless air
And open, honest, fresh, fair face and eyes
With their all-varying looks of pleasant surprise
And joyous interest in flowers and tree,
And poising humming-bird and maundering bee. . . .'
— JAMES WHITCOMB RILEY

The Grand Army Highway will lead us, if we wish to go, from the tip of Cape Cod all the way across the country to the Golden Gate. It follows Route U.S. 6 and crosses the Hudson River at Bear Mountain. From there, going west, the Highway brings us into the Palisades Interstate Park and on through one of nature's playlands. We cross the Delaware River at Port Jervis. Then we strike out into Bruce Lake State Forest towards Lake Wallenpaupack. We are hardly out of Scranton when we see a highway marker pointing to Clarks Summit. There we stop.

We are looking for a college at Clarks Summit. A store-keeper from whom we seek directions informs us that we are looking for "The Venard." When we ask the old settler why he called it "The Venard," he simply waves us on and assures us that when we get there we will find a full explanation, better than he could give. They always called it "The Venard," he says, ever since he could remember, and he well remembers when the place was started over thirty years ago.

The directions are correct. The college is exactly where we were told it would be. A quick survey shows us a building that resembles in certain points the old Franciscan missions of El Camino Real. It is surrounded by a great variety of shade trees, orchards, pasture land, gardens, baseball fields, handball courts, and a beautiful little lake with a dam at one end testifying that its present size and depth may be owing to the ingenuity and patience of man. Activity hums about the place, but not on the play fields. Boys in old army clothes or dungarees are pushing wheelbarrows, wielding pick and shovel. Some have hoes or rakes, and all are engaged in what seems to be hard manual labor.

Inside the building there is the usual layout of classrooms and dormitories, dining hall, science laboratory and a beautiful chapel. In the chapel our Guest Master brings us to a red-draped shrine and we learn at last the complete story of why the college is called "The Venard." It is named after a French boy who studied at the Foreign Mission Seminary in Paris, was ordained to the priesthood, and sent to Indochina where nine years later he was martyred for his Faith. The story of his short missionary life was brought to America by a priest, ordained at Paris with Venard, who had to flee from France during the Communist revolt in 1871. His letters, read to the students at St. John's Seminary, Brighton, Massachusetts, kindled a spark that grew into a flame and started a movement which in time brought about this college and others like it. From this college hundreds of American boys have followed Venard's footsteps to the East. But it is better to start at the very beginning.

Jean Theophane Venard was brought up in the farmlands of western France, in the Department of Deux Sevres, near the Vendée. He was born November 21, 1829, the day on which the Church commemorates the Blessed

Virgin's entrance into the Temple service at Jerusalem. His father, a retired schoolmaster, acted as Justice of the Peace in the little village of St. Loup and cultivated a bit of land on the upper edge of a beautiful valley known as Airvault, which is a corruption of the old Latin name meaning Golden Valley.

One of his boyhood chores was to tend his father's goats. Late one afternoon, when his father joined him and his companions on the hillside that they might walk back to the village together, Theophane asked the elder Venard abruptly: "How much do you think this field is worth, Father?"

"I am afraid that I do not know exactly," his father said, puzzled by this unusual question. "Why do you ask?"

"Because," the boy answered, "if you could give it to me, and I could have it for my share, I would sell it, and then I should be able to go to college and study."

His father, surprised at such serious thoughts in one so young, put him off with some simple answer; but he thought over these words which gave him a new light on the character and intentions of his son.

Among the books which Theophane borrowed from the pastor of the village, to read while tending the goats, were the Annals of the Propagation of the Faith. He and his companions had just finished reading the report about Father Charles Cornay, whose martyrdom was then recent. He was impressed by the detailed account of the priest's sufferings and death, and he said aloud: "I am going to Tong King some day, and I, too, am going to be a martyr!"

His father allowed him to take up Latin at the priest's house along with some other boys. Theophane succeeded so well that it was decided to send him away to boarding school.

He was twelve years old when he left home for the

school at Doué, which is about fifty miles to the north. He was a good student and a good schoolmate. He put his mind seriously on his books during study time, and at recreation he threw himself with all his heart and energy into the games. He bore all ill-nature and boyish contradiction with such good humor that those who at first were inclined to tease him soon gave it up. It seemed that the more people annoyed him, the harder he tried to be kind to them. He rarely failed to win them over, and then naturally they were ashamed of their previous behavior.

He entered into all the little private devotions of the students. He had a special devotion to the Blessed Virgin since childhood, instilled by his mother who was a gentle pious woman with a beautifully simple and loving character. He seemed in all things to combine the gentle virtues of his mother with the firm resolution of his father.

So far as he was permitted, Theophane tried to discipline himself with little practices of self-denial. When, on a winter's day, one of the teachers seeing him suffer from chilblains on his hands and feet, told him to go and warm himself by the fire in the instructor's room, the boy refused with thanks, saying, "The missioners you were talking about last night, sir, suffered much more than that."

He liked to read. He preferred the lives of young saints, and especially those who had suffered matyrdom. These holy dispositions were fostered by the thoughts of his First Communion which was approaching and for which, though still but a small boy, he was trying to prepare himself with the utmost care. He wrote home to keep his family posted on his progress: "The most beautiful day of my life will soon be here, the day that I have been looking forward to so much. Please pray to Our Blessed Mother for me, that I may receive her Son worthily. I feel that I can never prepare myself enough for such a big occasion. Please pardon anything wrong I may have done, all my faults against you, and give me your blessing."

He had his previous doubts and fears, but when the time came his joy knew no bounds. That was the beginning of his great devotion to the Blessed Sacrament. One of his teachers said: "I used to open the door of the chapel softly just to see if he was there, and I was always edified by his wonderful attitude. He seemed to be completely aware of God's presence. Sometimes I forced him to go out to play with his companions, as I thought it necessary for his health. Then he would realize that obedience came before any personal devotion."

A great sorrow was hanging over his head. Returning to school after his first vacation at home, Theophane knew that his mother, then very weak from a long illness, could not live much longer. He was not sure that he would see her again. Very soon after, in fact, she passed away peacefully. To the boy away at school the blow was terrible. Nevertheless, his first thought was how he could best console the mourners at home.

"Dear Papa," he wrote, "when your letter came telling me that my darling mother was very weak and suffering, I flattered myself that our prayers and tears would move God to leave her with us. But just now our principal has come to tell me of our sad loss. I beg God to help me say: Thy will be done!

"The hour fixed by Him has come, and she has had to leave us and is gone to be our protector in Heaven with the two little angels to whom she gave birth. Again, may His Holy Name be blessed. It is thus that He tries His creatures here below. Our faith, our religion is our only comfort in such sorrow.

"But it is very, very bitter. I have cried till I can cry no longer, and I have prayed with all my heart for her dear soul. May she at this moment be enjoying the presence of our good God with His Saints. May the Savior whom she ever loved and whom she strove to serve, receive her into His Kingdom."

From the time of this great sorrow, the links which bound him with his sister, Mélanie, were drawn closer, and a correspondence began between brother and sister which ceased only with death.

Their letters are models of tenderness, while they are most attractive in point of style and expression of holy ideals. The old Bishop of Poitiers, who was fond of reading these letters, used to say: "It is in this outpouring of heart to heart that we see his extreme delicacy of feeling, his loving thoughtfulness, his graceful imagination, and the good judgment which balanced all his other qualities. We have read these letters again and again, with ever increasing pleasure, and we trust we shall be forgiven if we have watered some of them with our tears."

One of these letters to his sister was written during the winter of 1844: "I must send you a few lines, for there is not a day, nor scarcely an hour, when I do not think of you, who are so very dear to me. I know you, too, are thinking of me, and I suppose you will be saying: 'Oh, my poor old brother must be so cold this winter, and here I am enjoying a good big fire!' Don't worry about me, sister dear. I have found the cold somewhat trying, as you know I always do, yet I have had some fun out of it too. We had grand skating. Now the weather is milder, and I am beginning to thaw out, and as I thaw, I am pouring out some of my thoughts to my dear little sister, my second self."

Soon after, his younger brother Henry joined him at school. He took the small boy under his wing and tried to spare him some of the usual schoolboy troubles. About the same time he was assigned the charge of the school chapel and sacristy. This was an honor which he prized greatly, and it gave him more opportunities to be near the altar.

"Yesterday," he wrote to Mélanie, "I went to say my Rosary in the chapel; and I don't know why, but I was very sad, and I began to cry like a child. Yet all the time I felt a wonderful comfort in my heart.

"Very often, when I am at work, my thoughts fly back to you. I seem to see you going lightly about the house, singing softly as usual, and doing things for our father and the children and everybody. I follow you in thought everywhere. Although we are so far apart, our thoughts, our wishes, our aspirations seem to be one. Oh, what a blessed thing it is, this communion of souls, to be able to pray for each other, and to pray for our loved ones together! A sort of peace and calm comes over me with this thought.

"Do you know, the other day, on the Feast of our Patron Saint, as I was kneeling before the Blessed Sacrament at Benediction, the Blessed Virgin seemed to smile amidst her flowers and tapers, and I thought of you, who, I know, were then at the Sodality Vespers. I prayed so hard for you, and I felt that you were doing the same for me and that our prayers were one. And then I was so happy, so relieved. But I should like to be with you again in body as well as in spirit.

"When shall we no longer be separated? When shall we be able to live together as we did as children and share all our troubles and all our joys?"

College Days

> *"The least insight that one can obtain into sublime things is more desirable than the most certain knowledge of lower things."*
> — THOMAS AQUINAS

American soldiers landing in France in 1917 disembarked at St. Nazaire, at the mouth of the Loire River. That was before the American army developed the harbor facilities at Brest and built a connecting railroad to carry troops and supplies towards the front. From St. Nazaire those first divisions traveled overland along the Loire to Angers and thence eastward. Just below Angers, in the same department of Loire, the college of Doué was located, and it was there that Theophane Venard spent six years of his preparatory training. American boys know that the winters in France can be extremely uncomfortable, even though the temperature may not drop so low as in some parts of the United States. This is especialy true where there are no modern heating facilities. Such was the situation in Venard's day.

"Here we are in the midst of piercing frost and cold," he wrote to his father on New Year's Eve, 1847, "but if the winter numbs our limbs, at least it does not freeze our hearts. Whatever happens—whether my chilblains disappear or not—I can't let New Year's pass without scribbling a few lines to repeat once more my hearty prayers and wishes for your happiness. People say that New Year's Day is the day for telling lies. Let those say so who tell them.

As for me, I always welcome this occasion for renewing the
expression of my old childhood love. In one word, dearest
papa, I wish you many, many happy New Years."

At this time Theophane was eighteen. Although he had
given himself up to God from boyhood, he was filled with
doubts and temptations when the time came to decide on
his vocation. As usual, he told his sister of his troubles:

"My dearest Mélanie, we must talk a little of the Blessed
Virgin, for I feel as if I had not spoken enough of her this
year. Can it be that I have changed? I think not; but other
thoughts preoccupy me just now. I am nearly at the end of
my classes here and yet I seem to have no clear concept of
my future. This worries me. I always thought I was called
to the priesthood. Sometimes I say to myself, 'What a
glorious thing it is to be a priest! What it must mean to
say one's First Mass!' But then for that, one must be so
good, so pure! Must be like one of God's angels. That is
why I still hesitate. Please pray with me that I may know
God's will. Remember me and this problem at your Communion the first Sunday of Lent, and I will do the same."

Peace came back to his soul. Again he had to tell Mélanie about it. "Once more I thank you with all my heart,
that's all I can say. Here is the month of Mary nearly over.
We, too, have special devotions every day for Mary's
month, and I love to decorate her altar. We have ever so
many beautiful roses in the garden here. The largest and
sweetest, you may be sure, I keep for our tender, good
Mother, and it is a great pleasure to offer her fresh ones
every morning. I fear that the hands and the heart that
bring them are miserably unworthy; but she is so good,
she receives everybody. Well may we call her 'Comfort of
the Afflicted' and 'Refuge of Sinners.' "

Mélanie likewise had to make up her mind regarding her

own vocation, and the difficulties which both met and the entire confidence which they had in each other bound them, if possible, still more closely. In Theophane's mind his sister appeared more and more holy. "You may be quite sure," he wrote to her, "that I am true to my promise, and if you pray for me I feel often as if my life were one prayer for you. But though you will laugh at me for saying so, I can't help sometimes, when I am asking God and His Saints to enlighten us, I can't help wishing for something that you do not want . . . but I will never try for an instant to turn you from any generous or holy project. I wish only for your highest happiness."

He gave his sister an enthusiastic description of the Corpus Christi procession, and concluded: "If religious services on earth are so glorious, what must they be in Heaven? Have you ever thought of that word—eternity? Eternal—something that will never, never end! It just overwhelms me to think about this. Then I wonder how I can still be so giddy and thoughtless."

After his six years at Doué, Theophane left for the junior seminary at Montmorillon. Those who were with him in school described him as a good-natured boy, pious and gifted with good judgment, frank in his manner. He was not tall, but rather under medium height. His hair was dark, almost black, and his complexion was clear, slightly tinged with red. His appearance was altogether pleasing; one enjoyed meeting him and talking with him.

His piety was not offensive. He was usually cheerful, with a good sense of humor, and no one could object that there was anything gloomy about his religion. He enjoyed good fun, yet everyone knew that he had a strong groundwork of serious deep feeling.

When his youngest brother, Eusebius, went off to school

he wrote him: "Well, how do you like school? Are the lessons hard? Disagreeable? Keep up your courage: you're at the bottom of the ladder now, but you will soon be climbing, and you will notice your progress.

"Are there any fellows there that you like? Do you have some fun? Tell me all. I wish that I might be with you during these first weeks of school . . . Right now it is six-thirty in the evening. I suppose the wind is blowing through the chinks of your door. It's bitter cold, isn't it? I'm sure that your little toes and paws are all chilblains, as mine used to be. And the tip of your nose is frozen stiff, isn't it? That's life for you—real schoolboy life! So we learn, and we learn to put up with things.

"But let's forget the winter and wish each other a Happy New Year! Every day will be New Year's by and by, when you are in Heaven. But I don't hope for that just yet, as I don't feel quite disposed to give up my little brother so soon. Remember how we used to look forward to New Year's in the good old days, but you were looking for presents then, and for some good things to eat. No presents and goodies now, only class work and home work. Oh, dear! But by and by you will know lots of things and be able to fulfill your life's work better, as appointed by God, and that is the way you will win Heaven. That alone is the object of what we do. Work hard, work well, not for praise, not for honor, or prizes, but just to please God. Take this as your life's maxim: 'All for the good God.'

"Don't forget your prayers now. Do as your superiors say, for they are set over you by God. Be good and kind to your companions, and everybody will love you, and you will be really happy. Good-bye."

When Theophane finished his courses at the junior seminary, he was to be advanced to the major seminary at

Poitiers, but first he had a vacation at home. He looked forward to this trip and made his plans with those at home.

"In another month I shall see the sky of my own native valley. What a happy thought! My friends at the Major Seminary are beginning their vacation a month earlier, and that makes me a little envious. The time will soon slip by.

"My schoolboy life is at an end; it has not been without its trials, but it has had its happy moments, too. At present, I feel as if I need the fresh air of my own dear home to strengthen me, body and soul. Till now I have not *lived*. I am going to begin.

"Every living thing seems to follow its vocation. The river flows to the sea, the plant takes root, the animal feeds and grows, man lives and draws daily nearer to God. But each man follows his own way. The business of one is to cultivate the soil; another, the intellect. Handicrafts supply the material wants of mankind. One and all gravitate towards their end, which is death, although each follows a different path. In one sense man has a free will, but he can scarcely be said to choose his career; it is almost always marked out for him. If he wanders from it, confusion may result. Well, I am longing to work and to find my place in the world, to work for the happiness of others.

"Whatever course be proposed, I always come back to that—to be a Priest. No other career has the least attraction for me. Yes, one day I shall be a soldier of Jesus Christ, and fight under the banner of the Church, and that day will soon dawn. That is why I feel so happy at the thought of going home soon. A week or two among my own people, and then back to my studies and to my vocation forevermore."

The vacation came and went, and his letters were soon

arriving from Poitiers telling about his new life there. "In my room everything reminds me of something. I love every inch and corner of it. Everything about it seems to tell me of something good to do. I come in; to the right is my holy water font, and it seems to say to me: 'Your room is your sanctuary; nothing impure must enter it,' and so I leave my worldliness at the door, and purify myself with holy water. I walk towards the window and look out on the sky, and I say to myself, 'Up there a place is reserved for you; work and struggle hard to win it.' Then I beg of Our Lord to bless my labor, and lest any strange thought should disturb my mind, there hangs my Crucifix, preaching forever by the Divine example. Then above my book-case, the Cross stretches out its arms and covers me with its shadow; and soon I shall have the picture of Mary Immaculate watching over her Child. You imagine that I may have some troubles in my present life, dear Mélanie? No; I do assure you this place is to me a paradise upon earth. Everyone is happy here, even those who, like me, are far from being saints!

"How good you are to me! And how I love you for your tender thought of me! I said, 'I want some sleeves,' and in a trice here they are! 'I should like a curtain for my window,' and there it hangs. I wanted some money, and behold, here it is, without my asking, as well as half a dozen minor things which make my little establishment complete. Only one thing is lacking and that is time! A little quarter of an hour to say, 'Thank you!' and again 'Thank you!' "

"So my news troubled you, dear little sister, did it? I told you simply about one of the seminarians leaving for the foreign missions. But is there anything so very extraordinary in the fact that one among us is going to devote himself to the salvation of the heathen? Why, one talks of go-

ing to be a Jesuit; another, to the Trappists; another to
China; and so on! If you think there are no events and
no gossip in the Seminary, you are very much mistaken.
But you have created a whole world of hopes and fears out
of that one little sentence of mine! I can scarcely help
laughing. Another time don't let your imagination run
wild, but sleep in peace."

At the end of his first year at the seminary, just before
going home, he drew up some resolutions for the holidays,
which summed up briefly were these: 1. I will get up the
moment I wake, offering my heart to Jesus and Mary, and
never sleep later than six o'clock. 2. I will examine my
conscience every day just before lunch with a short medita-
tion on faith, or charity, modesty, spirit of prayer, and so
on. At the end of the month I will make a general review
to guard against relapses. 3. In the course of the afternoon
or evening I will go to church for a visit to the Blessed
Sacrament, bringing along a book of devotions. 4. Directly
after breakfast I will spend an hour at study. In the evening I will study again a little bit. 5. In dealing with others
I will try to be careful in what I say, I will be gentle and
kind towards everyone and especially towards my own
family. If the opportunity presents itself, I will manage to
put in a word about God, especially if I am with children.
I must always remember, however, that deeds are better
than words. I can alter this rule if necessary, especially if
my companions insist on my going with them for a walk
or an outing. I will take care to avoid anything singular;
all affectation is tabooed. True merit is hidden and simple
and dreads public notice.

All this time, of course, he continued the seminary practice of Mass and the Sacraments. Every evening the family
gathered to say the Rosary together, and while he was

home on vacation he was usually asked to lead the Rosary.

Another year passed, and Theophane was home again. He spent almost the whole time with his family. He helped his brother to make a little grass terrace at the foot of the garden, where, he told himself, after his departure they might sit and think of the absent one whom they had given for God's work.

He was now close to the end of his seminary studies and the time was drawing near when he would have to make the definite final decision on whether or not he intended to go on for the priesthood. He wrote to his father to secure his formal consent. Then he was raised to the order of subdeacon with which he was to begin his final year of preparation and with which he assumed the obligation of remaining single to devote his whole heart and soul to the service of his Lord.

All this time his letters continued, and one of them to Eusebius was a little lecture on piety. "Don't think for an instant," he said, "that you have to put on a sour face; and don't think that you have to look sanctimonious. True devotion is natural, and happy, and bright, according to the words of Saint Paul: 'Rejoice in the Lord always; again I say, rejoice!' "

After receiving the order of subdeacon, he wrote again to Eusebius: "Henry IV said, 'Hang thyself, brave Crillon! We have won a victory and thou wert not there!' So I say too: you were not there when your poor old brother, prostrate on the floor, gave himself forever to God. But I know it wasn't your fault; so please don't hang yourself. Just help me to thank Our dear Lord for His goodness to me and for all the joy He has given me."

Meanwhile, Theophane had written to the Foreign

Mission Seminary at Paris telling of his hopes to be a missioner. The reply came back, accepting him. He began to prepare for Paris.

Theophane's departure for the Paris Seminary was definitely settled. He had to break the news to his family. His father, proud of his son, had already made many plans for his future. Theophane knew this; and although he thoroughly appreciated his father's courage and generosity, yet he shrank, as his favorite child, from inflicting a blow which, he well knew, would put an end to all his father's hopes. Nevertheless, he could not bear that anyone else should give the news, and so he summoned courage to pen the following letter.

"February 7, 1851

"My Dearest Father,—A little more than a month ago, you came to witness my consecration to the service of God. You yourself, as it were, presented the victim at the altar. A poor and miserable offering indeed! Yet such as it was, Our Lord in His infinite mercy accepted it. And since that moment how the time has flown! God guides the hearts of men, and they follow as He leads. God took me by the hand, and spoke to me. 'My son!' He said, 'come, follow Me, fear nothing; you are little, and poor, and weak, and miserable, but I am the Almighty God. Come, I will be with thee!' And I, can I have any will other than the will of God?

"My dearly-loved father, do you understand what I am trying to say? One day God said to Abraham, 'Take thy only-begotten son, Isaac, whom thou lovest, and go into the land of Vision; and there thou shalt offer him for a holocaust upon one of the mountains which I shall show thee.' And Abraham obeyed without a moment's hesitation, and without a murmur; and his obedience was most pleasing to God. Now, my dearest father, do you understand? Here am I, the child whom you love; I have not asked anyone else to break the news. I am telling you this myself, simply and frankly. God calls me; yes, it is His call. You, please, call me likewise; say that you, too, are willing that your Theophane should be a missioner!

"Poor father! There, I've said it: the *Foreign Missions.* Do not shrink from the thought. Rather kneel and take your crucifix, that crucifix which received my mother's last breath, and say, 'My God, I consent, may Thy holy will be done. Amen.'

"Father, forgive me for having struck the blow myself! Some people will tell you I am mad, ungrateful, a bad son, and I know not what besides. My darling father, you will not think so! I know you have a great and generous soul, and one that has drunk deeply at the only true source of real strength and greatness—that of Religion and Faith. I have saddened your heart; my own is sorrowful and heavy, too. The sacrifice asked of us is hard—most hard! But, O Lord Jesus, since Thou dost will it, I will it likewise, and so willeth my father.

"Courage, then, my dearest father—courage, and resignation and confidence in God and in His Holy Mother. Let us pray for each other. Father, I kneel at your feet. Bless your child, and believe in his respectful devotion and dutiful submission."

As he knew beforehand, this letter struck his father as a thunderbolt. Nevertheless, M. Venard was a large-hearted and generous Catholic. His answer was a consent heartily given. One day, when a friend was trying to console M. Venard by assuring him that his son's vocation had been abundantly weighed and proved by his superiors before they gave their assent, he exclaimed, "And what would become of the prophecy of Our Lord Jesus Christ, who declared that His Gospel should be preached throughout the whole earth, if directors of colleges and heads of families were to check the aspirations of all the young students who wish to go to the foreign missions?"

Such was the generous nature of the father as shown in the following letter:

"*St. Loup, February 12, 1851*

"My dearest, well-beloved Son,—I will not attempt to describe the emotion your letter caused me. I fancy you had calculated beforehand the force of the blow. You may well say that the sacrifice is hard. Your ordination cost me nothing. On the contrary, it fulfilled my fondest wishes for you, and I was quite content. But now everything is changed. All my plans are upset. Well may people say, 'Man proposes, and God disposes.' I had flattered myself that you would some day have a parish near me, that I should be able to make over everything to Henry, and then come and finish my days quietly under your roof, so that you should close my eyes. Happy, but alas, hopeless illusions.

"My child, I cannot attempt to turn you from your great and holy resolutions. Neither will I sadden your heart by reproaches. I will content myself with asking if, at your age, you think you can really arrive at so serious a decision, and not regret it hereafter. But if you are resolved, if you feel that God has indeed called you, then I would say, 'Obey Him without hesitation.' Let nothing keep you back, not even the thought of the poor old father whom you leave in his sorrowful desolation, nor of the paternal roof which will no longer shelter you. Enough; I know that he who puts his hand to the plough must not look behind him; I know also that he who leaves father and mother to follow his Lord will receive an eternal recompense, and such reasons are unanswerable . . . I could not reply to your letter at once, my dearest son, for poor human nature would have its way at first. But today I am a little calmer, and I hasten to fulfill your wishes. You ask for my consent. I give it to you without restriction. My blessing, too, I give you, my dear boy. How could I ever refuse it? You know that I belong only to my children, and that you may always reckon on me. All that gives you pleasure gives it to me likewise, cost what it will. My sacrifices began when you first went to school and I was separated from you; they went on increasing year by year, and now God knows where they are to end! Well, I can only resign myself and leave all in the hands of Him who, perhaps, will give me back my Isaac, to use your own comparison.

"Do not let my letter sadden you. I cannot put my ideas down as I wish, but you will guess my thoughts. Let us hope that God will sustain us both in this great trial. Although your sister knew of your intention beforehand, she was terribly affected by your declaration, for she felt that the day was still far off. But, as you say, the time is short . . . Henry saw at once that there was something the matter, but I have told him nothing as yet. And poor little Eusebius, whom you were to mould and form, is he to lose his model and his guide? Forgive my saying this—forgive your poor old father, who lives but in his children. I feel I have gone too far, and that I shall give you pain, and you don't deserve it.

"Bear in mind, then, that I freely give my consent to your plans. Be at peace, and do not trouble about me. The

hand of God is everywhere. I love you with all my heart
and embrace you tenderly."

Theophane went home for a vacation of two weeks before leaving for Paris. He knew that he himself, and all at
home, would have a hard time restraining their emotions,
but he felt that he owed this visit to his family. There were
many unforgettable moments during those two weeks. In
the evening by the fireside, after the dishes were put away,
they would sit together. Often there would be a dead silence, the father contenting himself with pressing his son's
hand and not daring to trust himself to speak. Theophane
would try to cheer them all by droll stories, or interest
them in the countries he was so soon to visit. He excited
them so much on the subject of China and the missions,
that nothing would content Mélanie and her brothers but
the thought of going too. They made a thousand little
plans, in which each was to share in his labors. "And what
is to become of me?" asked their father, who had been
listening in silence. "Am I to be left like poor old Zebedee
to mend my nets? Rather than that, I will go too." Indeed
he several times told his son that nothing but his duty to
his other children kept him back, adding that he had no
longer anything else to bind him, and that all he asked of
God was to be allowed time to launch his children in life,
and then sing his "Nunc Dimittis."

So the days sped on, only too rapidly, and each evening
became more sad as it grew nearer to the last farewell.
Poor Mélanie felt the strain especially, and every night
would linger after the others to get the last kiss and the
last word. There was always something more to say and
the last night of all they made no attempt to retire. Mélanie had several little things to add to his outfit; and he

sat watching her, saying as many loving things as his sad heart would allow. Ten years later, Theophane, then a Confessor for the Faith, recalled every single incident of that night. Only two days before his martyrdom, he wrote from prison to his sister, "It was alone with you that I passed that delightful night of the 26th of February, 1851, that night at home which was the scene of our last interview on earth, spent in holy, helpful, consoling talk like that of St. Benedict and his sister."

The day of departure came at last. This was the last time the family would be together, since it was understood that after his ordination at Paris Theophane would depart directly for the missions without returning home. Travel in those days involved too much difficulty, and the family could not think of making the long journey to Paris to be present at his ordination and departure. So, it was his last day at home.

The whole family sought strength where alone it could be found, and received Holy Communion together. Theophane served the Mass. Then came farewell visits to friends and relatives, when he tried to turn aside sorrowful thoughts by a bright, gay manner, and occasional little jokes; yet he admitted afterwards that he was nearly choked with sorrow. One visit cost him many tears—it was to the churchyard, to the grave of his mother, whom he had so idolized, and from whom he had been separated at the hour of her death, so that he had never had her dying blessing—to him a cause of continued regret. He could scarcely tear himself away from those precious remains. And yet the thought of this visit was most consoling to him afterwards, and he always spoke of it with deep gratitude.

The hour of departure was fixed for nine o'clock in the evening. Theophane had chosen that time to avoid a crowd of sympathizing friends; his brother and one old friend were to drive him to Parthenay, where he would take the night train. The family sat down to dinner earlier than usual, the good old pastor of the village having joined them; and Theophane, by almost superhuman efforts, succeeded in making the meal cheerful, almost gay. But a few words from his father towards the end brought back sad thoughts and they all became more and more silent.

The dinner was over and the time of departure was drawing nearer. As usual they said the Rosary together, then read a chapter from the *Imitation of Christ,* after which they knelt for evening prayers. No one had the courage to lead except Theophane himself, and as he went on the sobs and tears of his little audience became more pronounced. Theophane with difficulty finished the prayer, and approaching his father, said: "It's time to go. We'll have to say good-bye. Father, give me your blessing, please." As he spoke, he knelt at his father's feet. The poor father lifted his eyes and his hands to Heaven, and with a broken voice, making the sign of the Cross on his child's head, said: "My dearest son, receive the blessing of your father, who offers you a willing sacrifice to Our Lord. May you be blessed forever and forever, in the name of the Father, and of the Son, and of the Holy Ghost. Amen!"

Theophane knelt for a moment in the same way for the good old priest's blessing, and then rapidly kissed his whole family, as he did each evening before going to bed; but this was for the last time. Henry went out to see if the carriage was ready. Eusebius threw himself into his brother's arms, sobbing as if his heart would break. Mélanie kissed him a final farewell and fell back fainting. The poor father, silent and motionless from excess of sorrow, leaned heavily on the arm of his old friend, the Curé.

"Courage! let us be generous in our sacrifices!" murmured Theophane. He could bear no more. With one last kiss to his sister, he seized his cloak and hat, and rushed into the carriage. Several friends and townspeople crowded round him. He shook their hands, saying: "Good-bye! good-bye! we shall meet in our true home." The carriage set off rapidly for Parthenay.

The sacrifice was over and M. Venard, without wronging his other children, could say, "I have lost the fairest flower in my garden!" The delay at the moment of departure, though slight, made them miss the train at Parthenay by five minutes. This was a very real trial for Theophane, who longed for the final parting to be over. But there was no help for it, and so he and Henry waited for the next train, which started at six o'clock in the morning. His brother remarked that when once settled in the railway carriage, Theophane looked away, and burying his face in his hands, cried uncontrollably.

CHAPTER THREE

Au Revoir

> *"We meet again one day in Heaven's*
> *land of blessings—*
> *Farewell, Brothers, farewell!"*
> — Missionary Departure Hymn

Three days later Theophane was received into the Seminary of the Foreign Missions, in the Rue du Bac, Paris.

"I was hardly in the house," he wrote home, "when I was greeted graciously on all sides. Every kindness was showered upon me. One took my trunk up to my room. Another untied the cords. A third made up my bed and showed me around the building. A fourth introduced me to those in charge, and then brought me on a tour of the garden. In a half hour I felt as if I knew them all as old friends. This grand welcome certainly did my poor old heart good; it had been bursting with sadness since saying good-bye to you. There is nothing in the world like the kindness here and the way they make you feel at home right away. We are all like one big family, with one object and one aim."

Diaconate, the last step before the priesthood, came at Christmas in 1851. "The ordination was very large," he wrote. "All the different communities of Paris were represented. I found, kneeling side by side with me, Vincentians, Dominicans, Franciscans, Holy Ghost Fathers, seminarians from Ireland, and even some from Africa. I knew none of them; but my heart went out to them with love and sympathy, for I knew that we are all children of the same Father, servants of the same Master, soldiers of the same King."

As the time for his ordination drew close, everything about the seminary seemed to help him prepare. The atmosphere of the place strengthened his ideals. In a corner of the seminary garden there is a little oratory dedicated to Our Lady. On Saturdays and on the evening preceding feasts of Our Lady, the oratory is filled with flowers and its candles lighted, and the students gather to sing hymns in her honor. Each evening after Night Prayers, before retiring to their rooms, the students pay a visit to the Hall of Martyrs, a large room in which there are relics of former students who have suffered for their faith, together with the instruments of their torture and pictures representing their martyrdom. The students pray here for a few minutes in silence.

Theophane used to spend many spare moments in this room. When news came of the martyrdom of Father Schoeffler in Tong King, he wrote to his sister: "I would love to give my life for the faith some day, just as he has done. I am not afraid of saying so to you, because I know how generous you are; you would not want me to lose the martyr's crown. The Tong King mission is the most attractive right now because going there means almost certain martyrdom."

Theophane wrote to the Bishop of Poitiers to remind him that the time of his ordination to the priesthood was drawing near and that soon thereafter he expected to leave France for some distant mission. "I admit that every day I get more and more detached from France, and my tastes have become decidedly Chinese. I do not know what it is that attracts me so towards these people of other climes, be they Indians or Chinese. Some of my friends tell me that

I am getting to look like them, that I have a Chinese head, Chinese eyes, Chinese ways, in fact, that I am becoming completely Chinese.

"Don't think, however, that I have my heart set upon China. I am ready for any mission my superiors may pick for me. I shall always be very happy in the place where our Great Master may allow me to work for the glory of His Holy Name and the welfare of my brethren."

His superiors recognized his merits. They advanced the time of his ordination, and though he was only twenty-two years old, they told him to get ready for the ordinations on June 5th. He sent the good news to his Bishop:

"Fruit that ripens before time has not much flavor. Here I am, young fruit and green, and I am supposed to ripen and be ready in only one month. Even with this hot May sun, isn't it too much to hope for in one month? I never dreamt of being called to the priesthood before Christmas, but God has disposed otherwise.

"Very soon perhaps another message will be brought to me: pack your things and start. Yet when I look at myself, my hands of a mere boy and yet called to receive the holy oils, my feet better accustomed perhaps to the play field and now called to carry Our Lord's words of truth and peace to faraway places, my whole self just beginning to understand what life is and yet called so soon to teach men to live. It almost makes me laugh and at the same time I feel like crying. My thoughts right now are so mixed that all I can do is ask God to give me all the strength I need, with meekness, humility, prudence, knowledge, charity."

Theophane was ordained to the priesthood at Paris, June 5th, 1852. He had been down with a severe illness but recovered sufficiently to take part in the ceremony. The next day, Trinity Sunday, he said his First Mass. He wrote to his father: "Send me your blessing, dear Father. I said my First Mass today. What a glorious day! My head is still weak and I cannot meditate very well, and so I can hardly realize the wonderful mysteries in which I may now participate. But I feel a great peace, and I am very happy. You will all share in my joy because it belongs to all the family. I wish that you might have been here for the ordination, but God arranged otherwise. At least we are always united in prayer."

Three days after his ordination on June 5th, Theophane was told he would soon depart for the missions. The destination was not yet announced. He would have a month's notice before the actual sailing. In September he received the news and wrote home immediately.

"September 13, 1852

"My dearest Father, Mélanie, Henry and Eusebius—Once more let us say together, 'God's Holy Name be praised!' A month ago, five of my classmates were told to be ready for departure. I was left behind to build up my health. I was disappointed, naturally, but we can skip that part now. One of the five, who had to go home for family affairs, could not return on time. So—I am to take his place. I am leaving right away. This is just to say 'good-bye' until we all meet in Heaven. Friday this week will be my last day in France. We are sailing from Antwerp." Six days later, departure day, he sent a short note to each of those at home.

"My dear Father—Today I leave France. I am sending you this last note of farewell. We start at seven o'clock. On Monday or Tuesday we sail from Antwerp. Good-bye, dear Father. This separation is hard for both of us, but let's have courage. Life here passes so quickly. We will soon be together again in Heaven. Au revoir, dear Father. With all my love—good-bye.

"My dear sister, my own little Mélanie—Good-bye. I feel it very much that I am not able to write you a good long letter. This hurts, because there are so many things to tell you. I shall never forget our happy childhood together, all the joys and the get-togethers of our happy home. By and by we shall all be together again. I confess that I am leaving with a very heavy heart; but let's be brave. God bless you. This note must carry my last kiss to my dear little sister.

"Dear Henry—Good-bye. I enjoyed your last letter. No, my heart is not made of stone; right now it is melting like wax. We are going to meet again some day. I go now to bring word of Our Father in Heaven to our brothers who do not know Him. Pray for me. Only prayer can relieve bitterness and sorrow. Don't think that I can ever forget you. But let's have courage and fight our battles bravely. Good-bye. I love you with all my heart.

"Good-bye, Eusebius—We are about to be separated, but we shall be closer than ever in our thoughts and prayers. Let's keep going straight towards Heaven, no matter how rough the way. Happy those who get there first! We are starting for Tong King under the best of auspices; only yesterday we got word of a new martyrdom there. Once more, good-bye."

The Departure Ceremony took place in the Seminary chapel. It was in the evening. Theophane's family was not among the large group of relatives and friends who came to see the five young missioners for the last time. The directors of the Seminary and the students filled the chapel. A veteran missioner gave the departure sermon. Then the

young missioners stood on the altar steps while the others
present came forward to bid them Godspeed. It is the
custom in France to kiss the feet of the departing missioners while the choir sings the hymn, "How beautiful are the
feet of them that preach the Gospel of Peace, of them that
bring Glad Tidings."

A little incident is recorded of this departure ceremony.
An old man came forward from the crowd of visitors. He
walked with difficulty and was assisted by one of the
priests. A sort of hush fell on the chapel as all eyes followed him going towards the altar. He kissed the feet of
the first four missioners. When he came to the fifth, the
young priest bent forward and tried to prevent him. But
the poor old man knelt, or rather prostrated himself before
him, and lay his head on his son's feet, the soft white hair
covering them as if with a veil. A sigh burst from him,
more like a sob, heard all through the chapel. The son was
deathly white. This was the second boy given to God, and
it was his last. Friends helped the old man to his feet and
walked with him back to his place. The choir had paused
to watch the little drama. They continued with the psalm,
Laudate Pueri Dominum, and then on with the Departure
Hymn while the young missioners bade farewell to their
friends.

CHAPTER FOUR

Down to the Sea in Ships

"Ah, what pleasant visions haunt me as I gaze upon the sea!
All the old romantic legends, all my dreams, come back to me.
Sails of silk and ropes of sandal, such as gleam in ancient lore,
And the singing of the sailors, and the answer from the shore!"
— *The Secret of the Sea*, H.W. LONGFELLOW

The *Phylotaxe,* an American clipper ship, was at the dock at Antwerp when Theophane and his companions arrived to start for the East. The *Phylotaxe,* which means "lover of order," was a boat of 600 tons, small as compared with our present-day luxury liners of the Atlantic, some of them of fifty thousand and even seventy thousand tons, but it was an excellent ship for those days, a good, fast sailer. The missioners had to wait a day before the ship was ready for sea. They went sightseeing in the quaint old Belgian town and they made the acquaintance of the townsfolk. They embarked September 23rd. Theophane wrote home:

"We bade farewell to Antwerp with a salute of nine guns, which was answered from the fort. I find myself dreaming of home. I feel the separation keenly, especially when I think how long it is going to be before I shall have any word from you all. Anyway, you are *anchored* in my memory. You see, like a good sailor, I am beginning to use ship talk.

"We have already passed two nights on board, two beautiful nights at sea. The moon throws a soft light on the waves, and we walk the deck, singing our old songs, smoking our cigars. Yes, I am smoking now; we are ordered to smoke. A kindly gentleman at Antwerp gave me a supply for the trip—a thousand cigars, mild ones fortunately, which I survive much better than the strong ones. I sleep like a little bird in its nest, and I have not been sick—so far.

"It is a good comfortable ship, with a picked crew. The discipline is admirable. The Captain is like a father to us. We have a dispensation to eat meat on Friday but out of deference for the Belgian custom we abstained this week. The Captain never omits grace before and after meals. The other officers are just as faithful. The winds so far have been favorable.

"I am struck with the hard life of these sailors but I can see that it has a certain charm. I like to listen to their monotonous singing while they work away, and I hold my breath while they climb up into the rigging. But the wonderful expanse of water and the thoughts which it suggests, hold my attention most of the time. I wished good-bye to every village and every steeple as we sailed past. Now we see nothing but water and sky. Good-bye then for many months."

He was able, however, to send a few pencil lines the next day:

"Sunday, September 26, by a fishing smack,
seven leagues from Calais.
"My dear ones—One more word to say that I am well, though rather seasick. We are all bright and cheery on board. Pray for us. Dearest Father, Mélanie, Henry, Eusebius, once more good-bye! A last farewell to France and to you all."

In the normal course of events these would have been his last lines from Europe. A violent gale, however, forced the ship to seek shelter in Plymouth harbor. There it remained three days. Theophane gave his brother an account of the storm and subsequent experiences.

"This evening I was watching a beautiful sunset on the English coast while the moon rose on the French side of the Channel. I couldn't help thinking about England where the Sun of Truth has so long been darkened. I pray for this country with all my heart. England could do so much for the good cause if she would only make it her own. Britannia rules the waves but she sows error in the lands under her flag. Let us pray that all this may be changed.

"It must be a rare sight for English people to see a priest in his cassock, for when we went ashore, men, women and children looked at us in amazement. Some of the little ones were fairly frightened and ran away. One of the men was curious enough to touch the cassock and examine the buttons. Then they burst out laughing, and that so naively, that we laughed, too. Evidently they are very much like the Chinese in some ways, curious to the verge of incivility and with very little sense in their mockery."

To his sister he wrote a letter full of recollections of the happy days at home. "Do you recall how in the old times, when the summer vacation came to an end, you and I used to take the longest way around to the station? We could never agree who was to have the last word. We always had a lot to say to each other. Now I am leaving you, and it may be for ever. So shouldn't we have a good long talk? You are all together at home, and I am here all alone. But rather, I should say, I am alone with God.

"I know your thoughts have followed me and I can imagine the welcome this letter is going to get at home. I'm a real baby, don't you think, giving in like this to an attack of homesickness?

"But we are all going to be together again some day in Heaven, and then these few short years of separation will seem like nothing. Our mother and our friends have arrived there already. It's up to us to follow them. People going to the same place often choose to go by different roads. It's the same with us: I'm going one way, and you are going another way, and whoever gets there first must give the other a little help and encouragement.

"Mélanie, I am leaving you our dear old father. You will have to be his angel of consolation and make his last days on earth happy and peaceful. Keep an eye on our brothers, too. You can help them. Keep them together with yourself; three are always stronger than one. You can help one another upwards and onwards along the rugged path of life. Let nothing come among you that would diminish that strong bond of affection. Our Good Lord will watch over you to strengthen and safeguard that family love, and He will be the strength of all of us.

"Life has many bitter hours, sad and weary hours. At times, we feel it can scarcely be called existence. Our Father Who is in Heaven knows our wants, and He feels for our weariness. He is an ocean of love and mercy; in Him is all joy. We are like little rivers, and when we run dry we turn to this great source of life to send us the dew and the refreshing rain that our soul needs.

"Mélanie, when you hear the priest at Mass say the *Sursum Corda* (Lift up your hearts), think that it is I who am speaking to you, who invite you in Our Lord's Name to lift up your heart. Even on this sad earth, while we work here below, let us keep our hearts in Heaven. Climb high into the sky and look at the world as with the eyes of a bird, and then we will see things as God sees them, and sorrow will seem to fit into the plan of things. Pray for me and pray for those among whom I am going to work, our poor heathen brothers and sisters. In this way your prayer will be truly Catholic; this is the real communion of saints.

"I am counting on some long letters from you and I know already how they are going to cheer me up. Ask our old friends to do the same. Think what a letter will mean to me out there. I will dash off some lines for you in Chinese style, just for the laugh. Let's be bright and cheerful in our letters; the sad parts are all right in their place, but there is such a thing as too much, you know. Now I must come to a stop. A Dieu! You understand? God bless you, dear sister!"

From Plymouth he sent a few lines to his brother Eusebius: "Thanks be to God for the wind and the rain and the storms that have blown us into this town of Plymouth. It gives me another chance to write a word or two to Eusebius. We have already said good-bye, and our lives will henceforth run in different channels, unless you acquire a Chinese taste like mine. Though I left you, my heart is still with you.

"You are going back to college. Work hard. Time is precious. Learn all you can, and especially learn languages. People get around much more than they used to do. This interchange of ideas ought to work towards the triumph of truth. Try to get into this work in some way. I leave you to the care of your Guardian Angel. May he watch over your youth and your whole life. We shall meet again in Heaven. Meanwhile, I give you the same advice I gave Mélanie, *Sursum Corda*. May God shower on you all

His best gifts, patience, peace and joy in this life and in the next."

Theophane's letters from Plymouth were dated October 7th. After a voyage of three months the *Phylotaxe* approached Singapore, and the young missioners knew that they would be soon at their destination. After another three months, in April, Theophane's first letters from the East reached his home in France.

"We are entering the harbor, so I will get some letters ready to send home. It will help me to celebrate today, New Year's Day. This morning my first thought, after God, was for you all.

"On Sunday evening, October 10th, we left Plymouth. Another ship left at the same time, a Belgian boat the *Atalanta,* with a hundred and sixty passengers aboard all joining in the gold rush. What a miserable goal. I wouldn't have left you and my dear home for all the gold in California and Australia.

"Our vessel is a very fast sailer. Our Captain is a perfect Christian gentleman, genuinely religious. He does not speak much, but when he does it is right to the point. He has his ship in perfect order. His courtesy and his kindness could not be exceeded. Obviously, he is popular with his men.

"The days at sea have been long and monotonous. There is very little change to create interest; now and then we see strange birds, sometimes a swallow, flying fish, porpoises, occasionally a shark, and that is all. The sea wearies me to death. It is a grand sight to see the big waves rolling and breaking, but I would much rather view it from *terra firma.*

"We had Mass every day for the first month and a half, but then our altar breads were spoiled. We have missed the Mass terribly. I long for the opportunity to make a visit to the Blessed Sacrament. We know what it means now, to say that the body without food languishes and dies; it is the same with the soul, without the Bread which sustains its life.

"Time and again during this trip, alone on deck, leaning against the bulwarks, I found myself dreaming of the days gone by—my happy childhood, my dear mother, my father's sacrifices, my days at school, our happy gatherings at home. . . . And now here I am in the hands of Divine Providence, full of thanks for past favors, full of hope for the future.

"My dear father, in your last letter to me, when you consented to my departure, you encouraged me with the words, 'The hand of God is everywhere.' From now on, this is going to be my motto: The hand of God is everywhere. It will be everywhere with me.

"When we reached Singapore we learned about the Empire being proclaimed in France. It was not a great surprise. God grant peace to our dear France.

"Here in this land it seems that gold is worshipped as the supreme deity. New mines are discovered day by day. I have not yet heard that men found peace and happiness in gold mines. Charity is the only pure gold, tried in the furnace. Anything else is just counterfeit coin."

Father Venard and two of his companions started for Hong Kong after spending three weeks at Singapore. While they were still in Singapore some students from Cochin China stopped there on the way to the seminary at Penang. Theophane was impressed by this first contact with native seminarians from that part of the world towards which he was heading. He wrote to one of his classmates:

"Every evening these young men pray together in their

own language. We get close to the door to listen to them. They sing their prayers, and the tones are so beautiful and plaintive. It is quite an experience to hear them. They are real heroes, too, these boys with us. A price has been put on their heads for leaving their own country. They are the sons of martyrs, the brothers of martyrs. They come from Annam, the land of martyrdoms."

CHAPTER FIVE

Hong Kong

"There is no strange and distant place
That is not gladdened by His face.
And every nation kneels to hail
The Splendor shining throught Its veil."
— *Citizen of the World,* JOYCE KILMER

A British sailing ship brought the missioners from Singapore to Hong Kong. It was a long tedious passage. Father Venard expected to find letters from home, but there were none, not even a letter from his sister, and this was a bitter disappointment. He was homesick for the first weeks. At last, the letters came. He wrote home at once to tell of his joy:

"Your letters did me so much good. They came like refreshing rain after the great heat of the summer. I felt just like a traveller in the desert who finally comes upon a beautiful green oasis and finds rest for himself and his camel with the cool shade and plenty of water. Now you know what your letters mean to me. They have made me so happy. I feel a thousand times stronger, and I don't know how many times I have read and re-read them. It is clearer to me now than ever before how much you are sharing this sacrifice with me, and so I do not feel so much alone. Thanks be to God for the wonderful home He gave me and for the family love which keeps us all bound so closely together."

He stayed fifteen months at Hong Kong. He knuckled down to the study of the Chinese language, a very difficult task. His health failed under the intense summer heat; frequently thereafter he had to interrupt his studies. He took long walks by the sea and into the hills. He wanted to know the people. Their pagan ways disgusted him at times, but the women, he learned, were far ahead of his own countrywomen in modesty and decency of dress.

What annoyed him most was the bad example of the Europeans in Hong Kong who called themselves Christians and yet "spoiled God's work wherever they went." The opium situation roused his special indignation:

"Opium is extracted from the poppy and is smoked somewhat as one smokes tobacco. The effect is a deadening of all the faculties of mind and body, a complete stupe-faction. The Chinese have a passion for this pernicious drug, and the British have an equal eagerness to supply them with it. They bring it from India. In spite of treaties and protests, this contraband traffic goes on, and the sums acquired are enormous. The trade is a disgrace to the English nation. If the devil had tried to invent something to ruin men's bodies and souls, he could not have hit on anything more effectual. I wish we could have an associa-tion of prayer to try to put an end to this infamous traffic.

"Nothing could be more terrible than the state of China at this moment. The sad part is that European agents are at the bottom of it all. They hope, by doing business with the revolutionary element, to promote a sectarian move-ment among the people. This is a delusion.

"Worst of all, this just increases the Chinese hatred to-wards foreigners. As a result, when the Emperor succeeds in putting down the rebellion, which is certain, his ven-geance will fall on the Europeans. The missioners, most likely, will have to bear the brunt of this.

" 'What are the rebellions all about?' you ask. Nobody

knows. The French papers and the English papers print long articles with startling descriptions of terrible battles that have been fought, and so on, with elaborate theories about the future of the Chinese Empire. These are all dreams, complete fiction without a word of truth, and every one laughs at them. The papers also tell about the wonderful things the British and the French are doing for Christianity. Pure fiction. The governments of today have drifted far from the spirit of Constantine and Saint Louis of France. They have become secular and godless under the impact of sectarian influence. Expediency is the rule. For our work, God alone can give hope. We are relying on Him while we work and pray for the salvation of these poor heathen."

"You ask me, dear old friend," he wrote to his classmate, Father Dallet, already a missioner in the field, "if you still live in my memory. Yes, you may be sure, you have a very special place in my affections. I prize your friendship as something very special, and since no one could possibly suffer by this particular friendship I feel confident that God does not disapprove of it. It is for Him and in Him that we are one heart and one soul.

"My Bishop wrote to me just before I left Paris. He said: 'I pray for you to Our dear Lord, that your devotion may daily become more perfect, and that having embarked upon so great a work, you may persevere in it . . . Do not be an apostle by halves . . .'

"Now I have these words always before me, and they have given me courage. I have copied them for you, too. Let's not be 'apostles by halves.'

"I can't help laughing when I think of you with a beard. And you think I envy you! No, I have a moustache, and that is quite enough for me.

"I can easily appreciate the difficulties you have run into in your mission. But it is always the same: gold must pass through the furnace. I am full of sympathy for you; the miseries you mention would make anyone's heart ache. I seem to see them and even feel them. Sufferings, however, are good; they have done me much good, and I believe they have given strength and maturity to my character. I know that they have brought me more vigor along with firmness and courage. After telling me all these sad things, you add: 'Happy are those who can keep themselves apart, and live with God in the peaceful silence of their own hearts.'

"Well, now I must stop. My heart would go on forever pouring itself out to you, but my head is tired and so is my hand. For both of us I repeat constantly this favorite little ejaculation: 'Jesus, meek and humble of heart, have mercy on us.' In fact, I say this so often that it has become a habit. I hear you saying: 'Oh dear, here comes another sermon!' No, you're wrong this time. I'm not going to give you any more bad advice: I'm simply trying to make myself a little more meek and humble. God bless you, dear friend and brother."

During his stay in Hong Kong, Father Venard taught Philosophy at St. Francis Xavier College. This college was under Father Guillemin who later was made head of the Canton mission territory and was consecrated Bishop at Rome. At that time, he visited France where he met Eusebius Venard and brought him news of his brother. Eusebius was then a student at the seminary of Poitiers.

"When I was made superior of the Canton mission," the Bishop said, "all the students of St. Francis Xavier College, with Father Theophane at their head, came to congratulate me. They recited some verses which he had composed in my honor. They even made a mitre and a crozier for me, all out of bamboo. His bright disposition was a wonderful help to me in running the college. The students idolized Father Theophane. He was largely responsible for the admirable spirit among them, and he showed them how to make light of all sorts of hardships. One day he went with me to a very high hill, from which he said he could see his 'Promised Land.' I never saw him so happy as on that day. Your brother is indeed a perfect missioner."

While Father Venard was still at Hong Kong there were new arrivals from the Paris Seminary. Among these was Father Chapdelaine. Theophane used to describe him as "a Norman with an iron constitution, full of life, open as a book, a perfect companion, the healthiest of us all, and likewise the most active and the jolliest, with the bloom of perpetual youth on his cheeks." Father Chapdelaine went to the missions of Kwangsi and after only two or three years his work ended in martyrdom.

In February 1854, Theophane received his assignment to the missions of western Tong King. He wrote at once to the Superior of the Foreign Mission Seminary at Paris:

"Tong King for China—I am not losing much by this exchange. I should have been glad to accept any mission assigned to me, but Tong King, with Bishop Retord, so full of holy associations, is really the post I wanted most. I love it. It is the grandest mission of all, 'the Diamond of Asia,' as some poet has called it. When I was still at Paris, left behind when my classmates had departed, Father Albrand used to say: 'Don't be blue; this isn't a case of *tarde venientibus ossa* (the late comers get the bones).' I like to think of this. Please extend my thanks to that dear, good Father for all his kindness to me." Theophane wrote also to his family:

"Well, my dear people, I am going to Tong King. That is where Father Charles Cornay died a martyr. I cannot yet say that I am going to have the same good luck, but perhaps if you pray hard enough, God may grant me the same favor. I am not going to China; I have seen it as Moses saw the promised land. My boat will take me to other shores, to a land where Father Schoeffler and Father Bonnard both won the martyr's palm, one last year and the other the year before.

"My destination is the land of the Annamese, which includes Tong King and Cochin China. Persecution rages there against the Church. A price is put on the head of each missioner; when one is discovered he is straightway put to death. God knows His own, however, and only to those whom He chooses is given the grace of martyrdom. One is taken and the other is left.

"In spite of the persecution, the missions there are most flourishing. It is clear that the 'blood of martyrs is the seed of Christians.' We run the risk likewise of being cut off by pirates on our way from Hong Kong to Tong King. But all that is in God's hands.

"The mission to which I am going is a large one, with over 150,000 Christians. It has 80 Annamese priests, and I will be the seventh missioner from the Paris seminary. The religious communities are well established and have more than 600 Sisters. Some of the work of instructing new converts is done by a corps of 1200 catechists. There will be more native-born priests; 300 students are in the seminaries.

"Then think of the martyrs that this region has given to God. They are the patrons and the protectors of the mission. Think what an honor it would be if your own Theophane should be among these. Wouldn't the words of the

Church's prayer of thanks mean much more to us all: 'Te Deum Laudamus . . . We praise Thee, O God. The white-robed army of martyrs gives praise to Thee. . . .'"

He wrote also to his classmate Father Dallet: "It is only a few years since Father Galy and Father Berneux went to Tong King and were seized by the soldiers as soon as they set foot in the land. If we could only be just as lucky! The thought of it gives me a thrill of joyful hope. But I suppose I should not dare to think of anything so brilliant; and yet I really long for such a favor. Don't forget our prayer for each other: 'Holy Mary, Queen of Martyrs, pray for us.'

Theophane wrote home again before leaving Hong Kong. One letter was to his brother Henry: "You say: 'Eusebius arrived hale and hearty, and so we are *almost* a complete family together.' I know what you mean. I may not be with you, but my thoughts are home, often. Never since I departed have I known the real family joy, but of course that was to be expected. . . .

"Don't think that I am blue. On the contrary, I am quite happy. Living for God and working for Him, we are rewarded with peace of heart.

"You say that you are busy all day scribbling on musty old papers. Well, I suppose office work has its charms, but not for me. Give me the wide open spaces. That hunting trip you wrote about brought back to me recollections of the good old days. Wouldn't I have enjoyed being with you! I do not know what Tong King holds for me, but I guess I will not be doing much hunting.

"Well, God is everywhere, and what more could we ask to make us happy. There is no sense in looking at the dark side of things. There is always a brighter side. We have our ups and our downs; everyone does, unless he is some sort of phenomenon. I guess it is just the struggle between the good and the bad in us. When the good is on top, we are in perfect peace. When we give in to worry and disgust, then nothing seems to go right.

"The right thing to do is to fight against any feeling of dissatisfaction. If we do not, our ideas will be all mixed up and our judgment will be unbalanced. The bad in us is helped to dominate by bad companions, bad books, carelessness in our work, and so on. Of all these, bad books are the worst.

"Bad books are the number one present-day plague. There are all kinds. The most apparent are those with indecent pictures and suggestive passages. More insidious are those filled with false notions, biased judgments, ridicule. Unfortunately, these books are sometimes composed with a beautiful style and rich literary figures which are very effective in destroying a healthy appreciation of good reading matter in the young. Pardon this sermon, dear brother. I know your passion for reading, and all I want to say is: don't play with poison."

A recent letter from his sister had mentioned the family's Christmas at home when, as part of the fun, they had drawn lots to see which figure of the Christmas Crib would be represented by the different members at home. Mélanie had drawn the name of Mary. The lot drawn for Theophane was marked "the donkey." He referred to this in his last letter from Hong Kong: "I am very happy with the role awarded me in your drawing. So I am to be the donkey. It's all right with me. I will just accept my part, and I am not accusing you of any 'fixing' in this matter.

"The donkey knows how to bray, and so I ought to be a good trumpeter for the Gospel. The donkey can take a beating without complaining. I will try to imitate his pa-

tience. Again, the poor donkey is scorned and laughed at;
his name is never used as a compliment. Still he goes about
his work and does it well. I am going to do the very same
and serve my Master good and faithfully everywhere, always.

"And you have drawn the name of Mary. Good. You
have chosen the better part. Guard it carefully. I can think
of you also as Mary of Bethany, sitting at the feet of Our
Lord and listening to His words. Yet I know you have
to be busy about the house doing the work of Martha.
Well, do the work of Martha with the spirit of Mary, and
then you will be imitating Our Blessed Mother, Mother
of Jesus, and you will indeed be perfect."

He left Hong Kong, May 26, 1854, with an older missioner who was returning to Tong King. They stopped
briefly at Macao, which is only a few hours' sail from Hong
Kong. Macao had been a great port but had declined with
the rise of Hong Kong. Ships of all nations were once
anchored in its harbor. It was the gateway to China. The
missioners who later gave their lives for the faith in China,
started from Macao.

"Portugal had a noble mission assigned to her by Providence," he wrote later, "but she misunderstood and re-
jected it. This brought about her downfall. It seems that
God broke her as one breaks a useless wornout instrument.
The kings of the earth have never been the winners in an
attack on the Church of Christ. Our Lord and His vicar
on earth can always claim the ultimate victory. This is
magnificently rendered in the Psalms: "And now, ye kings,
understand! Learn, ye who judge the earth!" Macao is
indeed a ruin.

CHAPTER SIX

Tong King

"Mother of Christ, and Mother of me
Save me alive from the howl of the sea.
If you will Mother me till I grow old,
I will hang in your chapel a ship of pure gold."
—*In A Boat*, HILAIRE BELLOC

"Father Legrand and I embarked at Macao on June 2nd, towards evening. We thought our Chinese captain was going to weigh anchor immediately. Not a bit of it. A Chinese will never do anything in a rush; make haste slowly, is his motto. They had to deliberate at great length over the many details of the voyage and the various contingencies that might arise, they had to consult the Devil, take proper precautions against attack by pirates, and so on." These details of the trip were given by Theophane in a letter to his brothers, Henry and Eusebius, which was dated June 23, 1854.

"We were to sail in a convoy with other Chinese junks. The skippers seem to mistrust one another and before actually getting away they made several false starts just to see if the other ships really intended to go and were ready to go.

"There we were, two poor foreigners, in the midst of a people who don't find anything to admire in Europe and the Europeans, and who are ready to bully you if you don't bully them first. Naturally, they found us timid and non-aggressive, and so we were thrust into a little low hole in the ship where we had to sit or lie down. The air was horribly foul, and we were covered with vermin. There we stayed day and night. If we ventured out of the hole, the sailors called after us 'Foreign Devils', and subjected us, with everything we had on and everything we did, to an unfriendly scrutiny.

"If there was a delay in getting away, if the wind was blowing in the wrong direction, if pirates threatened the ship, then *we*, the foreign devils, were to blame. It was impossible to please them. If we tried to be kind and friendly with them, they insulted us. If we kept by ourselves or said little, then we were called snobbish.

"The only thing to do in such circumstances is to take all these troubles and little crosses and to try to bear them bravely in the spirit of our missionary calling. Otherwise they would be unbearable. In this way, too, we can maintain a certain control of our feelings, which is an indispensable virtue here in the East, no matter how difficult it may be at times.

"At last, we set sail in company with seventy other ships. After a lot of parleying, the skippers had come to an agreement. Everyone realized that they had to travel in a convoy that would be large enough to frighten off the pirates. Six ships of the buccaneers' fleet bore down upon us when we were near Tin Pac, but we opened fire with the small cannon in our bows, and the pirates retreated. We then headed for a port on the island of Hainan and remained there several days.

"We did not dare go ashore while our ship was in port. We kept hidden. Father Bisch, from our own diocese of Poitiers, is working in the missions of Hainan island, but we didn't see him; the best we could do was to salute him with a prayer and unspoken good wishes.

"At Hainan our convoy broke up and from there on we

had only a small number of junks making the rest of the journey to Tong King. Until then the sea had been calm and beautiful. Afterwards the wind stirred it into a fury. I paid my usual tribute to the fishes.

"Two days later we sighted the shores of Tong King. It was a wonderful feeling to draw near to this land, something beyond words. Again I placed myself in God's hands, begged Him to use me for His honor and glory. I called upon our Blessed Mother to be with me, and I asked the same of my Guardian Angel and the patron saints of Tong King.

"It is a magnificent country. From the ship we had a good view of a luxuriant vegetation, such as you read about in Robinson Crusoe, with rich plains and green hills, and in the background a superb range of snowy mountains.

"We entered at the mouth of a beautiful river and then glided upstream. We passed through a fairyland of woods and gardens and at length dropped anchor near a place called Cua Cam, a booming center of contraband trade with China.

"During the day we were not allowed to leave our tiny cabin. Even at night we had to be very careful if we stole out on deck for a breath of fresh air. Fortunately, this lasted for only two days. The Custom House Officer came aboard to inspect the ship. We watched him through a crack in our wall, hardly daring to breathe whenever he passed close to us. He carried himself as a very important person, and, old fox though he may have been, he did not scent our nest and went ashore when the tour of inspection was completed.

"The next day we were smuggled ashore by a little company of Christians who rowed their boat alongside the ship, completed their bargaining with the crew, and then

hurried me upstream to the home of the Spanish Dominican Fathers. Nearly all the inhabitants of this area are
Christians. Bishop Hilarion Alcazar welcomed us as his
own and he is making me stay here to rest up from the
rigors of this voyage. His generous hospitality makes one
think of the early Christians of Rome."

At the end of July, Father Venard sent a letter to his
sister which continued the chronicle of those first days in
Tong King. It was dated July 31st and sent from Vinh Tri,
in western Tong King.

"You must have read my letter to Henry and Eusebius
about the trip from Macao to Tong King. As it turned out
later, we left the ship just in time. If we had delayed a few
hours longer, you might have received word of my death by
this time. Three ships of the native government surrounded the Chinese junk on which we came from Macao.
The rumor of our arrival had reached the authorities. Soldiers went through the boat searching for us, from top to
bottom, and then they went through the other junks that
had come with us. Escape would have been impossible. By
that time we were safe with Bishop Alcazar.

"We stayed with the Bishop eight days. I was ill the
whole time. An Annamese doctor fixed me up some kind
of tonic which had the right effect, and I was able to re-
sume the journey. Perhaps you are wondering what sort
of doctors and medicines they have here, imagining that
I am in a country of savages. You must remember that the
Annamese have a civilization equal to our own in Europe.
In fact, in some respects they surpass us. Their physicians
have genuine skill. The one who attended me simply felt
my pulse and diagnosed my case immediately as an upset
liver. I was soon able to travel.

"Our next stop was with Bishop Hermozilla. He is a

grand old Bishop, good through and through, simple and pious. One day, while we were there, a complaint was brought to him that the farmers had not paid up what they call 'the rice of the Blessed Virgin.' This is a sort of parish collection for the maintenance of the altars; each family is assessed a certain amount, and the whole project is put under our Lady's protection. The Bishop interceded on behalf of the poor people, since the rice harvest had failed that month, and he decided the case in their favor.

"We stayed two days at this episcopal *palace*. Don't let the name mislead you. A Bishop's residence here means a poor cabin, half wood and half mud, thatched with straw. The houses are all of the same kind. They are needed only to protect you from the sun and the rain, and they fulfill their role satisfactorily.

"The churches are not much more elegant. They consist of a straw roof which is held up by wooden pillars. On festive occasions, these pillars are draped with silk, and that is the extent of the splendor. The altar is made of ordinary boards. If the Church here could enjoy any kind of peace, even for a time, more elaborate churches would be built. Right now it is hardly worth while constructing anything but temporary buildings, because of the recurring bursts of persecution.

"We started out for what is known as the Central Vicariate of the Spanish Fathers. We were to have gone by water, but the wind was against us. So we made the trip in hammocks. This will sound strange to you, but it is a common mode of travel here. Two strong men are at either end of a stout pole which rests on their shoulders. From this pole hangs a covered hammock in which the traveller rests while making his journey. It is not quite so comfortable as you might think, especially if the trip is long, as it was in our case. Our purpose in choosing this mode of travel was to escape notice while passing through pagan villages.

"It must have been fair day in one of the villages which we passed. A great market stood by the roadside. We were just in the middle of this fair, when we came upon the house of a mandarin, the great man of the place. Now, it is a rule that all travellers, unless of superior rank, shall go on foot as they pass in front of these residences, to testify their respect. We did not dare to conform to this usage and thereby show ourselves to the crowd. Our bearers quickened their pace to a trot. Presently came the cry after us: 'Who are those people that do not get down from their nets?' The teacher, at the head of our escort, replied that we were 'sick people of his household.' 'At least, then,' replied the sentinel, 'let them lower their nets.' Our porters had to obey.

"Father Legrand, who knows the language, was getting alarmed. I, in my blissful ignorance, had no idea of what was going on and did not realize the danger. When the hammocks were lowered I thought that we were supposed to get out and I was delighted with the chance to stretch my legs. The porters, luckily, did not give me time, but hurriedly raised us up again and trotted on. What a prize the pagan soldiers would have found if they had peeked in on us.

"Soon after that we came to a river, and that was the end of the journey by hammock. We went into one of the boats manned by Christians and we were brought safely to the home, or hut, of Bishop Diaz who is in charge of the Central Mission of Tong King. After a few days' rest we bade good-bye to the Spanish Fathers. We had enjoyed their cordial hospitality at every stop of our journey to date. Now we were headed for the final destination, the mission of Bishop Retord, of our own Paris Missioners. Two messengers had already arrived from Bishop Retord to accompany us on this last leg of the journey.

"We started out by night, going in a boat. We were hardly under way when we had to pass a fort where there was a garrison of four hundred soldiers guarding one of the king's rice granaries. As we came alongside the fort, we were hailed and told to identify ourselves. The crew replied that we were mandarins on official business. The sentries suspected something. We heard a roll of drums sounding the alarm, and immediately a boat put out after us. The wind was with us, fortunately, and we had a good start on them. A second boat behind us was carrying more of our party and our baggage. The military caught up with this boat, but our attendants put up a brave front and fought them off. This will give you an idea, dear sister, of present day travel in Tong King.

"We travel mostly by night, because of the greater security. Sometimes we go by boat along the rivers and canals, continually changing from one boat to another. At times we go by sedan chair, or by hammock, as I have already described. Again, there are times when we have to go by foot, walking barefoot along the narrow dykes that separate the rice paddies. In the daytime this foot travel through the rice fields is not too bad, but at night you are always slipping to one side or the other and find yourself up to your knees in muddy water or even measuring your length in the mud. It is a very picturesque mode of travel, don't you think? It can be somewhat tiring, but we are rewarded with many good laughs; you can imagine the pretty figures we present after a night of promenade along the Great Mudway.

"Bishop Retord was preaching a retreat to his seminarians in preparation for ordination, when we arrived on the 13th of this month. His coadjutor, Bishop Jeantet, was there, too, and two missioners had just arrived. We brought the number up to six, which is an unusually large gathering of priests in Tong King these days. We had a real happy get-together and spent the evening singing all the old songs.

"I forgot to mention that all my belongings were carried off by the pagans. They left me nothing, so I am really as poor as a church mouse, and that is, an Annamese church mouse. But what do we care? I love these maxims of Saint Teresa:

> " 'Let nothing disturb thee!
> Let nothing affright thee!
> All passeth away;
> God only shall stay.
>
> Patience wins all;
> Who hath God needeth nothing,
> For God is his all.' "

In 1596, a great cross was found by the Dominican missioner, Father Diego Advarte, on the shores of Annam, now called Vietnam. It seems to have prefigured the history of missioners in Tong King. The Church in that land, always under the shadow of persecution, may be said to have grown with her head on the block, and her children's feet steeped in blood. Some 100,000 Catholics have been killed for the Faith in this country. Of these, more than 70 martyrs have been beatified, among whom are 26 priests. The cause of beatification for 1,300 others has been begun.

The first great persecution was in the eighteenth century. It was followed by twenty years of peace under Prince Gia Long, and the Church enjoyed a breathing spell in which it gathered vigor to withstand the frightful persecution of Minh Menh. This tyrant was a monster in human form rivalling Nero in his cruelties. The persecution raged from 1833 to 1841 and ended when Minh Menh was killed by a fall from his horse.

The new king, Thien Tri, weary of the bloody edicts of his predecessor, passed an act of amnesty annulling the penal laws. After a reign of only seven years, Thien Tri died and was succeeded by Tu Duc.

During the reign of Tu Duc, famine, cholera, typhus and other plagues decimated the people of Tong King. During these public calamities, the Christians went about among the sufferers, caring for the sick, burying the dead, and in many ways showing the charity of the Church in action. Their generosity was bestowed on everyone without distinction, including their former persecutors. Even so, the mandarins, who still hated the Church, worked on the gullibility of the people and said that the many catastrophes were signs of vengeance wrought by the deities who were displeased with the growth of the Christian religion. Thus they fanned the flame of a new persecution in which many lives were sacrificed.

A temporary peace followed this persecution, and during this lull in the storm Theophane Venard entered the country. His lungs had been affected during the long months of travel and he was still suffering when he reached Vinh Tri. He wrote about all this to his father:

"When I wrote to you last I was with Bishop Retord at Vinh Tri. At the end of August the Bishop sent me to a college at Ke Doan to study the language of the Annamese. He assigned me two teachers who could speak a little

Latin. The first month of study went like lightning. On the second Sunday of October I got up enough courage to preach a short sermon in the little church, and after Mass the village elders came in to congratulate me, not so much because they understood part of my talk or got any great benefit from it, but simply because they are so wonderfully thoughtful and polite. Although I made such a hash of their language, they felt it was the right thing to do to come in and encourage me.

"A few days after that I fell sick. There was an epidemic going through the College, and I was one of the first victims. Everyone was most kind to me. As soon as I could stand up and walk around, I went for a change of air to another village, Ke Dam, where an Annamese priest is in charge of the parish. Please note: *I went by boat across the fields.* Every year at this time there is a flood. The rivers overflow with the tropical rains that have been soaking the mountains to the west. The whole country becomes one vast sea. Most of the villages are under water.

"On All Saints' Day I was well enough to say Mass. The night before, on Halloween, the whole village gathered at the rectory to congratulate me on my recovery. The elders, dressed in their Sunday best, escorted me to the church in solemn procession amid the music of native songs and cheers.

"The very next night, that is the evening of All Saints, the people came to wake me and beg me to pack up and flee. The mandarin was on his way to search the house. It was mainly a rumor, but I felt I should do as they asked. I packed up everything in a jiffy. The men carried me on their backs in the dead of night, and we reached another village safely. This was my first flight by night, but since then there have been many others.

"While still away in these villages, trying to convalesce and at the same time trying to keep out of sight of the officials, I had a relapse. On New Year's Day I was so ill that I could hardly receive the people when they came to wish me a Happy New Year. The Bishop sent me his own doctor. His medicines helped me, but only for a time. I was ordered to observe absolute rest—no Mass, no Office, no hearing of Confessions, no reading or writing, and practically no talking.

"Father Castex, who was taking care of me, suggested that we make a novena to the Sacred Hearts of Jesus and Mary. We made it together, beginning on February 2nd, Feast of the Purification. At once I felt myself getting better, and now all the symptoms have disappeared. My strength is almost back to normal. Naturally, I am most grateful to Our Lord and His Blessed Mother and to dear Saint Joseph.

"About this time the political outlook was getting dark. A rebellion broke out in Tong King. A royal edict denounced our religion. Informers betrayed the whereabouts of the priests. The college of Ke Vinh was broken up. Bishop Retord and his priests had to go into hiding. The mandarin of the capital attacked the seminary at Ke Non, but Bishop Jeantet had already left for the mountains. He wrote back: 'I have been looking up my old haunts in the caves where I lived during the persecution of Minh Menh. It's not easy any more for an old man like me to scramble up and down these rocky mountain sides. I sometimes wonder how I manage to get on at all.'

"Father Castex and myself have been running from one village to another. We finally went into hiding near But Dong where we have been living like hermits, together with two of our professors, for the last two months. We hope, however, to come out soon as the storm seems to have subsided.

"We have to be careful because the informer who failed to catch Bishop Jeantet has offered his own head to the mandarin in case he cannot deliver a foreigner into his hands by the end of the year. So all of us stay alert. What will happen, God knows. In any case, it is better to hope than to fear.

"Bishop Retord writes to us: 'Jesus and Mary will not abandon us now any more than they have done before. Let's pray with great confidence and never be discouraged or give way to sadness. If any of us should win the martyr's palm, so much the better. *Not my will but Thine be done.*'

"The rebellion goes on spreading. The revolutionists say that they want to reestablish the ancient dynasty. Misery is widespread. Last year's rice harvest was bad enough. This year in many places it is lost. Thousands of people are dying of hunger. It is most pitiable. People in Europe have no idea of the plight of this unhappy land. The New Year's celebrations, which are ordinarily so gay, were passed this year in sorrow. There is no reason to hope that things will be brighter by the end of the year.

"But now, dear Father, I must stop. Adieu. Don't worry about me. What God keeps is well kept. Stay well. Pray for me. May the joy of Our Lord Jesus Christ fill your heart forevermore."

CHAPTER SEVEN

Night Journey

"Simon Bar-Jona," Jesus said
"Lovest thou more than these?
These have relinquished the land of their birth,
To preach My Name to the ends of the earth.
Sacrifice measures their love's true worth.
Lovest thou more than these?"
— MARK A. CHURCHILL

"The whole country is an immense sea at this time of the year when the floods continue for four or five months. The little green villages seem to float on top of this sea. Everyone goes by boat, and so do I. You should see my little boat, made of bamboo and very light, just big enough for one person. In the evening, after nightfall, I make the rounds to visit my people. Often I meet one of the men or boys en route, and then we have a race. Needless to say, your poor brother is always beaten."

Father Venard wrote this letter to his sister from the college at Hoang Nguyen (pronounced Hwong Yan). It was September 1857. His frequent reference to floods is explained by the fact that his missionary territory was in the delta of the Red River. This part of Tong King is somewhat like the delta of the Nile.

A glance at the map of Indochina will show that the country is divided into Vietnam, Cambodia and Laos. This whole area has about twenty-five million inhabitants. Vietnam in turn is also divided into three: Tong King at the north, Annam in the center, and Cochin-China in the south.

Vietnam is sometimes represented as a coolie's carrying pole
with its load at either end: Annam is the long narrow pole
with Tong King as a rice basket on one end, and Cochin
China as the rice basket on the other end.

"So you would like to be a little bird to fly this way and
see how I am getting on," he wrote to his sister. "Well, I
really like these people. The Annamese are good, through
and through. They love their priests. Till now, however,
everything has been so upset and I have known so very
little of the language, that I have not done very much
parish work. We are having a little peace at the moment.

"The elders of the village come often to see me and
they always have some little present. At first all I could do
was stammer a few words of thanks which must have been
completely unintelligible to them because I could see they
had a hard time to keep from laughing. They kept a
straight face. They are so polite, and for all the world they
would not want to hurt my feelings.

"The farmers come, too. The father of the family may
bring me the head of a pig killed for the marriage feast
of one of his children. A mother will come to ask prayers
for her son who has been taken into the army. Others
come with fruit. Some come to get a rosary or a crucifix. It
is a custom here that no one should call upon a superior
without bringing a present. If they catch an extra fine fish,
or if their gardens should produce some fruit or vegetable
larger than usual, they take the greatest delight in offering it to their priests.

"You have asked me about the Sisters here in Tong
King. They are Annamese women living together in a com-
munity. They are received very young, but take no vows.
They work in the fields, spin cotton and they *sell pills*.
This may make you laugh, but by going about the villages

with their little medicine kits they meet the people, speak of their faith, and are thus enabled to baptize dying infants.

"They live a life of genuine poverty. They are most sincere about their devotions, practice austere penances and they fast far more than ordinary Christians. They are invaluable as couriers, especially in troubled times, when they carry messages from one mission to another and pass undetected. They fit in well everywhere, since there is nothing in their dress or manner to excite wonder or suspicion among the people of the country. On long trips they always go in pairs. Like all Annamese women, they are accustomed to toil and fatigue and when at work they often carry great loads. They are loved and respected by the Christians who always call them '*Sisters*'.

"These people as a rule sing their prayers. I really think they do not know how to pray in silence. But the native prayers are beautiful, sung in soft plaintive melodies, with little musical patterns that repeat themselves. They have different tones for the litanies of Our Lady, and an especially delightful one for the litany of the Immaculate Conception. Best of all are their prayers after Mass, prayers of thanksgiving that never fail to bring tears to my eyes. Even if only one person has received Communion, he will chant his thanksgiving prayers aloud.

"They sing the High Mass very well. There is always a musical accompaniment with violin, harp and even drums, fifes and cymbals.

"The marriage ceremonies here are quiet and simple affairs, usually at an early Mass when all may receive Communion. There are no elaborate processions and no costly gowns for bridesmaids and so on. This will make you smile. I was to marry a young couple, the boy and the girl both about eighteen years old. They came for Confession and were to be on hand bright and early the next morning. The girl arrived on time, but the boy failed to appear. After a long wait, we told the girl to go home and come back the next day. Quietly and without question she slipped out of the church and went home. The next morning the boy was on time, and the marriage was blessed on schedule. Later in the day I had occasion to ask the boy what had happened. With perfect simplicity he replied, 'I didn't get up on time.'

"What about my Latin pupils? It is not easy for them since we are short of books. We do not bother to teach them Ovid or Horace or any of the heathen mythology. When their studies are completed they can usually read and understand the Catechism of the Council of Trent. They also study Philosophy in Latin."

The letters which Theophane wrote to his family during those years from 1855 to 1858 give a fairly complete and very graphic chronicle of what he and his people experienced—persecutions, flight, flood, crop failure, famine, sickness, intervals of peace. He was sick from March to September 1855.

"On Ash Wednesday I went to Father Castex who was at the College of Hoang Nguyen (Hwong Yan). It was only a short distance, but the road was bad, all mud and water. I took a violent chill. The fever got worse and worse. I had to flee by night several times to avoid the mandarins. These nights had to be spent in the rice fields and of course all this did not help to cure my fever.

"The others thought that my time had surely come. I received the last Sacraments. This was the second time I was anointed, but God sent me a doctor who got me up on my feet again. Bishop Retord has me with himself right now at Ke Vinh. He thinks he is going to complete the cure, but it will be difficult; my left lung is just about gone. I go into terrible sweats and there seems to be a great weight pressing on my chest. In the morning there is sometimes such violent catarrh through the mouth and nose that I cannot say Mass. Still my appetite is good, and I can study. Don't worry about me, please; just pray that I may make the best possible use of this sickness of my body for the good of my soul.

"The persecutions this year threatened to be terrible, but, thank God, they were not so bad as we feared. Our pocketbooks were the hardest hit. It took bars of silver to buy off the mandarins. Our poor missions have been bled white by these rapacious heathens. The people have so much to suffer. All they ask is a bowl of rice, and even this is denied them; it's one thing after another—greedy officials, floods, famine, poor harvest.

"In a way, the mandarins are the worst scourge. They are supposed to be the fathers and protectors of the people; instead, they are vultures preying on the people. If anyone should say that once upon a time there was an honest mandarin, I'm afraid I would have to doubt it. Christian villages make choice plunder. They may be accused any time of 'treason and rebellion against the regime,' and thus they become victims of extortion, and the sums must be large enough so that every official from mayor to provincial governor may get his slice.

"So far this year we have had no martyrs. One of our Christian doctors was thrown into prison with his two brothers. He is still there. He is an excellent man. During the Minh-Menh persecution he stood up for his faith and persevered under torture. I have not had a line from any of you since January, and here it is September.

"I am dying out like a candle," he wrote a little later, "and holding to life by a mere thread. I think the doctors have given me up. Still I am glad to accept whatever God wills. This may be the last note you will receive from me. Pray for me, that, though my body is failing from day to day, my soul may be saved through the merits of Him Who died for me. We shall meet one another in a brighter and better home. Adieu!"

He did not die. By December he had recovered sufficiently to write home again and tell of the peace the country was then enjoying.

"We are in a period of peace, more or less. Our schools have re-opened. The Bishop can officiate in public on feast days. We may walk in the college gardens, even *in the daytime,* and this is something that you would appreciate more if you had been, like us, cooped up for so long in one little room without daring to speak or sing above a whisper.

"There was plenty of excitement lately when a British warship dropped anchor at Touranne, near the capital. The plenipotentiary minister of Queen Victoria came with the Governor General of Hong Kong to negotiate a trade treaty with the Annamese Emperor, Tu Duc. Our 'gracious sovereign' would not receive the visitors. The British had to withdraw, their mission a failure. The consequences were disastrous for us, for we were accused of sending for the British. Thus it goes.

"We have had no news from home for more than a year. I try to be patient, but every time the courier comes and brings no letters, it is a fresh disappointment. Please pray for me that I may not let these things get me down and that I may become always a more worthy priest of Our Lord Jesus Christ. I am praying for you all the time."

After a year and a half, he still had no letter from home. Meanwhile news of the Crimean War reached them, and they also learned that Pope Pius IX had proclaimed the dogma of the Immaculate Conception. He mentioned these in his letters to the family, and told how his people welcomed the news about Our Lady. Then came more dark days.

"Since my last letter the persecutions have been renewed. One of our native priests, Father Huong, has been martyred. I accompanied the Bishop on one of his visits through the diocese. We celebrated Holy Week and Easter at Ke Vinh, and everything went off beautifully and peacefully, if we can use that word now. Perhaps you wonder how we can celebrate these feast days peacefully while we live in hiding, with a price on our head, constantly on the *qui vive.* But it seems as if we were under the special protection of God and Our Beloved Mother, that we might 'serve Him without fear.' We are like mice, stealing out of the hole now and then to catch a little bite, cat or no cat, and then hurrying back to cover at the signal of danger.

"We all spent two weeks with Bishop Retord and Bishop Jeantet at Ke Vinh, the end of June. We made a retreat together, and when it was finished we had one of those good old get-togethers with plenty of songs and story-telling. Then, best of all, came letters from home—after nineteen months!

"The letters brought us news of the allies' success in Crimea, the peace, the joy of all nations over the new dogma of Our Lady. We also received word of the embassy sent by the Emperor of France to negotiate with the ruler of Annam to stop the persecutions.

"We were just on the point of breaking up and going

back to our missions when there was a tremendous flood, the worst in the memory of man. We had to stay where we were. It lasted for a month, the waters breaking the dykes in many places and submerging four provinces.

"The newly sown rice was lost. The crop that was ready for harvesting was nearly all lost since it rotted before it could be rescued. Villages were destroyed, thousands of persons lost their lives. Some took refuge in the mountains. Others camped on top of the dykes. We took up the flooring of the Bishop's house and made a higher storey near the roof, which had to be pierced to let in air. The water kept creeping up on us.

"In the villages, which are hit annually by these floods, provision is made with a system of boats to save the people and supply their wants. But where there are no such precautions the misery is frightening. Gardens are destroyed, trees killed, livestock drowned.

"Working day and night, our students built a dyke sufficiently strong to save the church, but the Bishop's house was full of water.

"In the midst of all this I fell sick again. I had a high fever and an attack of asthma. While I was down with one of the very worst attacks, your letter arrived. What a joy, and what a tonic! The sight of your handwriting worked on me like the best of medicines. There was a very noticeable improvement in my whole condition, but just when I was beginning to feel good in a sort of convalescence I was laid low again by typhoid fever. This time it looked surely as if it were the end. Bishop Retord and the priests said Masses for me on the feast of St. Peter of Alcantara, to whom, St. Teresa says, Our Lord refuses nothing. I got better. I am up and about again but very weak. My appetite has come back. I hope to get back to work soon. My left side does not bother me so much now. God has kept me alive so far, and I hope He will let me do something for Him before I die."

His family felt that they would never hear from him again and daily they awaited news of his death. They had a glad surprise when a letter reached them in his own handwriting.

"At the end of the year 1856 everyone thought I was dying. So I took the advice of Bishop Retord and consented to a Chinese remedy which is used only in desperate cases, and is called in Annamese *Phep-Quenou* (pronounced *Fep Cunew*). It is something like cupping, or cauterization. Little balls of dried herbs, like absinthe, are placed on various parts of the body where they are ignited and allowed to burn. Chinese doctors say that there are three hundred and sixty places on the body which may be thus burnt. The thing is to know just which is the right spot to burn; otherwise you may be left lame, or blind, with your face disfigured, and so on.

"I was burnt in five hundred different places, of which two hundred were near the lungs. After a few days these cauterizations produced a little yellow pustule full of matter. This indicates that the operation was successful, as the system is supposed thus to eject all that is noxious. The result is that I am wonderfully better. For several hours I had to endure this miniature preview of Purgatory, but it was worth it. Enough of that; Bishop Retord says that I have chosen to specialize in ailments.

"One night in February, when we were at Ke Vinh, a villager came running to the Bishop's house with word that the mandarin of the southern province had surrounded the village with his soldiers and was going to seize us. The students led Bishop Retord into an underground hideout. Father Charbonnier and myself were stuffed into a narrow hidden passage between two walls.

"After four hours of breathless waiting in the dark, we were told that the danger had past. The mandarin went away but he arrested Father Tinh, an elderly priest in charge of the college. One of our catechists and the mayor of the place were also arrested. We learned later that in the neighboring province some Christians had been forced under torture to reveal where the Bishop was living. But this was only the beginning.

"In March the mandarin came back with his soldiers and destroyed the church and the college. We had been warned in time and were hiding in the mountains. Everything was in ruins when we returned. Since we felt that the neighborhood was filled with spies, it was decided best to get away from there for a time. Bishop Retord and Father Charbonnier went back to the mountains. I got a boat and pushed off in the dead of night for my old quarters at Hoang Nguyen, (Hwong Yan).

"When I reached the college I found Father Theurel there with Father Castex. The latter was worn out with this hard life and he soon became dangerously ill. Bishop Retord came down from the hills to be with him during this final illness. After great sufferings, Father Castex died on the eve of Trinity. We were always very close, and I feel his loss deeply. I hate to think of years ahead without him. The Bishop appointed me to his place at the college. I do not feel worthy to succeed him but I will do my best to copy his goodness and bring everlasting peace to as many souls as he did.

"Good old Father Tinh, who was arrested the night the college was searched, was gloriously brave before his persecutors. He was beheaded. The Christians were unable to get near enough to help him, but Father Tinh was always ready. When he received the death blow, the executioner's sword broke in halves. The mandarins thought this a bad omen and they ordered pagan sacrifices to appease the dead ancestors of the victim. Father Tinh's three companions were likewise steadfast during their trial. They were condemned to perpetual banishment in a distant, unhealthful mountain.

"Bishop Diaz, superior of the Dominican Fathers at Bui Chu, was denounced by the pagan official of the place, and now he is in prison. The mandarin there has a special hatred for all Christians and he has placed crosses at the gates of the town so that everyone coming in or going out may be compelled to trample them under foot. The Christians there have been subject to house visits day and night.

"The Emperor of France sent an embassy to plead with the ruler of Annam to put an end to the persecution. The mission was a failure, partly because the representative had no real powers and was escorted by unimpressive little boats. The king refused to see him. Christians and pagans alike had put great hope in the visit. When they saw how it failed, they felt that they had been let down and voiced their contempt for a world power that could do so little. This opprobrium has fallen heavily on us missioners. If France is going to meddle at all, she ought to take care not to start something that she cannot finish. When the ambassador failed to achieve his purpose, he threatened the king of Annam saying that he would be held to render an account for all the French blood shed in his dominions. That move did not help things one bit;

the king thereon imagined that we had sent for the French force, and when they withdrew they left us in the claws of the tiger that is more than ever infuriated against us.

"As a result of all this, a Christian official was seized with thirty of our people. They were tortured and then their sentence was read to them, condemned to be beheaded. The official was dragged through the streets of the capital. At every corner his sentence was read out, while he was clubbed. The sentence was full of blasphemies.

"I sometimes ask myself: Is God's grace no longer so effective as before? Is it too late to save these people? Are we missioners less zealous than our predecessors? It is heartbreaking to look around and see nothing but pagan pagodas, hear nothing but temple gongs, to see so much superstition to placate the devils. Our Lord has to yield place to the ministers of Buddha and Confucius. His priests live in holes and caves and a price is put upon their heads. When is it all going to end?

"The penal laws are cruel but they are only half carried out. The mandarins use them to extort money. It would not be so bad if you really could buy peace. Instead, this half-and-half persecution ruins everything and kills initiative. One day you build a church, open a school or college. The next week perhaps you have to run to the mountains and everything is destroyed. You might buy off one mandarin, and before you know it he is changed. The next asks double the price, which is impossible to raise.

"We are truly like exiles in a strange land under the yoke of the oppressor, but our hope is in Our Lady and we look upon the proclamation of her Immaculate Conception as a rainbow announcing the end of the storm.

"My health is improved, and the Bishop has given me a new district to look after with over twelve thousand Christians. Seven Annamese priests assist me. I am on the go most of the time, giving retreats, settling squabbles, confirming in places where the Bishop cannot go. On account of the constant persecution we cannot do very much in the way of making new converts, but we do what we can, and there are new arrivals all the time.

"After the Feast of the Assumption I went to a district almost entirely pagan. Only about two hundred Christians were scattered here and there. I tried to keep out of sight because the village was near the headquarters of the mandarin, and no European had ever been there before. Some little children, whom I had confirmed, unknowingly betrayed me by their chatter, saying 'A little foreigner has come to the village, very small, but very white and good looking.' You must understand that we Europeans pass for great beauties here on account of our light complexion. No matter how dark we may be we are considered light by these people whom the tropical sun hast burnt to a deep mahogany color.

"What to do? The alarm had been given. They would be looking for me. I put my trust in God and kept working. Day and night for a week I went among the people. The poor Christians were in a terrible fright. They stood watch all the time and turned away anyone they felt they could not trust. When I felt I had done all that I could for them, I stole away secretly by night and went to another village where there were more Christians and less danger.

"The floods this year have been extraordinary. At times my floor was under a foot of water. I had fishes, frogs and toads, crabs and water snakes in full and happy possession of my room. I was perched on some planks about three feet above them. What annoyed me most was that the rats insisted on installing themselves on my mat. One night in my sleep I rolled on one of them. It was a disagreeable experience, but on waking, I found a poisonous viper, with black and white stripes, which had likewise coiled up on my bed. He was asking for hospitality and hissed at me when I insisted that he get out. So I forgave the rat.

"I saw it would be necessary to raise my house. Some Christians helped me to build up a sort of dyke on which I perched my home, thus raising it four or five feet. The houses here, you know, are easy to transport. You have a light framework interlaced with a bamboo trellis, outside of which is a thin coating of mud. A coat of lime finishes the job. They are never more than ten or fifteen feet high. The roof is of dry leaves. So now I am high and dry and away from the water. I even have a little garden with roses, honeysuckle, balsams, and some stocks. Don't you think I am quite an optimist?

"Please don't go thinking that I am a great saint. I am not even a little one. Sickness has weakened me, dulled my senses, cooled my zeal. So you see my misery; please take pity on me and pray for me.

"My heart at times is just as cold as the tropical sun is hot. We have no beautiful churches here to lift our thoughts heavenwards. Pray for your poor brother that his soul may take strength. Ask also that God may give me a little better health; you know how the body reacts on the spirit. If the laborer stumbles in tracing the furrow, it will be crooked and only half done. Beg the Giver of all good gifts to give me what I need to do His work well.

"You asked if there is something I need for my church. If you could manage to make me a new chasuble I should be most grateful, and my teachers would be delighted. Only yesterday they said to me, 'Oh, Father, write to France and get a prettier set of vestments for Mass on Feast Days.'"

CHAPTER EIGHT

Under Fire

"Grapes in a crimson press in far Cathay
Offered, not immolated quite,
Needed the consummating act.—Ah they
Bled glad at sound of sanctus knell.
Fast, fierce feet the carmine wine press trod,
Trod till it seethed a sigh for God."
— EVERETT F. BRIGGS

The letters written by Theophane Venard in May, 1858, did not reach their destination. A report which Bishop Retord wrote at that time, however, makes it possible to follow the course of events.

"We are like birds on the branch of a tree," the Bishop wrote, "always on the alert, always getting messages that we have been spotted by the spies, that we have been betrayed, that the mandarins are going to raid our mission, that some Christians have been arrested, tortured, and killed on our account. To spare them this distress we hide in our boats, or in caves, and sometimes even in tombs up in the mountains where we run the risk of being buried alive.

"We spent eight hours in one of these tombs one day, getting air through a bamboo tube. When we finally got out we stumbled about in a daze, drugged by the bad air and the confinement. But the physical discomfort is nothing compared to the worries about our people lest they should yield and deny their faith under torture.

"It is almost impossible to escape once the soldiers get

on your trail. Only last week another of our Annamese priests was seized, thrown into jail and killed. His companions and pupils, all arrested at the same time, were sentenced to exile for life. Among them was a ten-year-old boy who refused to deny Our Lord though he was beaten unmercifully. At length they chained him like a criminal and he was ordered to wear the chains for the rest of his life.

"Our chapels are destroyed, our houses torn down, our students are scattered. Our money was wasted when we tried to buy religious freedom for our people. Father Theurel and Father Venard are with some of their people hiding in underground caverns. It is the same story with the others: Father Titaud's church and house were burnt before his eyes, and he escaped the tyrants by hiding in the jungle, hobnobbing with snakes and poisonous insects of all kinds; Bishop Jeantet, Father Saiget, Father Mathevon, Father Charbonnier and myself have had to do the same. We thought we could weather out the storm in our little hideout at Vinh Tri, but we, too, have now joined the bears and the tigers here in the mountains. Father Galy and Father Neron have escaped trouble till now because their mission is so far away, but I am afraid that soon word will come that they also have been driven away."

The Bishop then gives a description of the many ways by which the Christians were tortured. The persecutors used these devices to force confessions out of them, to betray the whereabouts of priests, or sometimes just to make them deny their Faith.

The instrument most used was the "cangue." This looked something like a ladder. Two wooden posts, about four or five feet long, were joined by four heavy iron bars, leaving the two sides about six inches apart. The weight varied; some cangues weighed ten pounds, others up to forty. This was dropped over the victim's head, so that he would carry the weight on his shoulders. To carry it for a few minutes would not be too bad, but to keep this thing on, day and night, for days on end, was absolute misery. The flesh around the neck and shoulders became raw. To increase the agony the jailers would drag the victims from side to side.

The prisons were a sample of hell on earth. The Christians were placed in stocks, in which the feet were caught just above the ankle. Often the boards of the stocks would be too tight and would cut the flesh. What made them more horrible was that the cracks in the wood were full of vermin which would be always sucking the blood of the victims. The stocks, of course, were immovable, and so the prisoners had to remain in the same position day and night, just sitting or crouching, never allowed to stretch or move about.

The "rotin," or knout, was the most brutal. Several prisoners would be laid flat on their stomachs in rows, one after the other, the feet of one being fastened to the hands of the next, and all so stretched as almost to dislocate their joints. Every blow brought blood and caused an involuntary reaction or start like an electric shock, so that those who were not struck suffered nearly as much as those who were. A certain interval was left between the strokes, and thus the torment lasted for hours, each victim getting fifty or sixty blows. For this the jailers used a whip, about the thickness of one's little finger, and nearly four feet long. The lash was split into four bits, firmly tied with twine and steeped in a hard gum which made the blows so much the heavier and kept the lash from softening.

The pincers were also used. Sometimes they were cold,

sometimes red hot. They kept a forge handy for this purpose. The jailer would seize a portion of the victim's flesh with the pincers, then drag and tear it off with a rapid twist. The victim meanwhile would be tied to stakes in the ground. This might be repeated five or six times. The pain was more intense if the pincers were cold, but the wound would heal more rapidly, whereas if the pincers were hot the pain would be felt less at the moment but healing would be much slower and the flesh around the burn would fester.

They had still another way to torture the Christians. They would force their victim to kneel on a board through which the sharp points of big nails were protruding. The nails would pierce the flesh right to the bone. This caused excruciating pain. It was the custom of the tormentors to mock their victim by ridiculing him, imitating his painful contortions and calling out terrible blasphemies.

Then the soldiers would try to make the Christians trample on the cross, dragging them here and there by the cangue, scourging them, ordering them to step on the figure of their Savior, and if the Christians continued to pray they were beaten on the mouth.

If they were still alive after all this, they were thrown back into prison, heavily chained and kept separated, one from the other. A heavy iron ring was fastened about their neck. Rings were placed also around their ankles and welded. Then the neck and the ankles were chained together, the chains weighing five or six pounds. If the chains were too long, the prisoner would have to carry them to walk; if too short, his back would be constantly bent. This description should help to explain why it sometimes happened, though rarely, that the victim's courage would fail and he would yield to the pressure of the tyrants and forsake his faith.

Bishop Retord said that beginning with Easter 1858 one misfortune followed another in his diocese and the whole situation oppressed him so that life had become almost unbearable. Only the special help of God kept him alive and at work. Writing to Admiral Rigault de Genouilly, who wanted an account of the state of things, he gave a graphic picture of the persecution and added:

"And now you ask what has become of us missioners here in a land that was once so prospering and full of promise? I can hardly tell you. It is more than six months since I have had word from Father Neron. Father Galy started for Manila to get help from the Spaniards, but I do not know what has become of him. He may have been murdered at sea like Father Salgot. Fathers Titaud, Theurel and Venard are in the mountains. I have not heard from them in two months. Bishop Jeantet is hiding somewhere; he was nearly drowned crossing a river the night he escaped.

"There are three of us here, one day hiding in a farmer's hut, the next day out under the trees, or deep in the thickets, scrambling up rocky roads, under the burning sun, in good weather and bad. We are half dead from hunger. Our clothes are in rags. Between fatigue and sorrow we are just about finished.

"For more than four months we have been unable to say Mass. We have no vestments, no altar, no cabin where we could be sure of a half hour's peace. Hardly any of our Annamese priests can say Mass either. What's worse, the sick die without receiving the last Sacraments. Our churches are destroyed, our people are scattered, we are all in hiding. Scarcely anyone knows where I am. I don't dare send messages. Letters to me are lost, because the people carrying them, fearful lest they be caught in the act, burn them."

In October 1858, Father Venard wrote home and told them that their letters written in 1857 and 1858 had finally reached him.

"You can imagine my joy on receiving these letters," he wrote. "I wish that in return I had some good news for you. Instead, there is nothing but misery to report for the past nine months. Some letters which we had written to the Christians of Nam Dinh were discovered when the messenger was arrested. Under torture he disclosed everything. He told his captors the location of the new colleges at Vinh Tri, Ke Non and Hoang Nguyen (Hwong Yan). At the same time, one of our people turned traitor and revealed the interior organization of the diocese, our hiding places and our means of escape when pursued. Father Theurel and I thought that by keeping perfectly quiet and out of sight we could stay on where we were. But the spies knew too much.

"In the middle of the night, June 10th, we got word that soldiers were on the way to encircle our neighborhood. Luckily, by this time everyone was used to sudden warnings and flights by night. Besides Father Theurel and myself, we had quite a group to get ready—three Annamese Fathers, fifteen teachers, more than a hundred students. We tried to hide most of the mission equipment. In two hours the task was done and we were on our way.

"When, at daybreak, the detachment arrived, two thousand soldiers in all, plus fifteen hundred young pagans of the neighborhood who were told to watch all the roads and possible avenues of escape, we were safely out of the way. Two of our students were caught. Later, when the soldiers came after us, they took ten more students who had been lagging. All of these they tortured and secured with a cangue. Among those taken was an old deacon, seventy years old. Subsequent raids on Christian villages brought them a total of more than fifty prisoners.

"They were put through all the usual horrible tortures. When one of our young teachers was told to step on the crucifix, he replied: 'If you were told to trample under foot a coin bearing the image or superscription of the Emperor, would you dare do it?' For this he was beaten. Another, when told to do the same, picked up the crucifix and addressed it: 'Dear Lord, You have never done anything but good, and these people want me to insult you! How could I ever have the heart to do that?' Twenty strokes with the terrible rotin was the penalty he had to pay for this outburst of piety.

"The officials ordered the students to chant their prayers. The boys began with the Litany of the Saints, and when they came to the petition about the enemies of the Church, they repeated with extra fervor 'Deliver us, O Lord,' and again when the invocations were chanted for the welfare of the Church, for Christian kings and rulers, for the confounding of its enemies, they sang 'We beseech Thee, hear us!' The mandarins got the idea and told them to stop.

"When they tried to compel a poor old woman with her daughter to deny her religion by stepping on the crucifix, the old lady said: 'Who would be fool enough to step on the head of his father or mother?' The judges were annoyed at being put in their place by the simple old woman. They sent her and the child back to their village.

"Three Annamese priests had been taken. They were beheaded. Two of our teachers and the poor old deacon died under torture. The rest were banished to a wild desolate mountain where others have gone before them and where others will surely follow them.

"The petty officials are real leeches. When they make an official visit they ask: 'Have the King's orders been executed?' Everyone knows that this means: 'Pay me, or there will be trouble.' The underlings are worse. They move in on the people, especially the Christians, and make the most unreasonable demands. If the people hesitate or are unable to give what is asked, they are arrested and jailed. The people have a nickname for them, 'Mandarin Horseflies.'

"Things are bad everywhere. It is difficult to get word back and forth because there are sentry blocks on the roads to keep the Christians isolated. We have a special sort of military police to pick up the Christians, and their most used device is to have a crucifix handy and order those who pass to step on it.

"The persecution has swept the whole country from Cambodia to China. The Spanish Dominican Fathers have had it even worse than we have. In their territory there is an order to execute all Christians by what is called the 'lang tri,' that is, a slow torture which is accomplished by chopping off the feet at the ankles, then cutting at the knees, the fingers, elbows, and so on till the victim is nothing but a mutilated trunk. Bishop Melchior, who was in charge of the missions of the Dominican Fathers in the eastern part of Tong King, suffered such a death last August.

"You will ask me: 'How have you managed to escape the storm?' Simply by the special favor of God Who has me in His holy keep and apparently has decided that my hour has not yet come. The Christians guard my cabin. All I have to do is hide in a little corner and keep quiet. The least noise, even a cough or a sneeze, might betray me. In these hideouts we consider ourselves particularly lucky if there is a little hole in the wall or roof for light, so that we may read our breviary and do some other useful reading.

"Cooped up like this we just have to learn patience. We learn also to trust in God. If there is probability of a spot raid, I should slip out after dark and hide somewhere else. At times it is safe enough to come out for a breath of fresh air and a few steps to stretch our cramped limbs.

"The saddest part of all is that we cannot bring the Sacraments to our people. Many of them die without the usual spiritual helps. Another annoying feature is that when we are in flight and take shelter with some Christian family, we nearly always compromise these poor people who give us hospitality. It is preferable for this reason to stay with friendly pagans because they are less likely to be suspected. Father Theurel and I stayed two days and two nights with one of these pagans. The owner of the house stayed away so that he might truthfully say he had seen no European. In the middle of the night we got a mysterious warning to get up and flee. We did so, and fifteen minutes later the place was raided.

"Bishop Retord advised us to take to the mountains. We hid in the caves once used by Bishop Retord and Bishop Jeantet. Here, too, we were betrayed. Soldiers were led to the place, guards placed at all the mountain passes, but again we escaped, although everything we owned had to be left in the caves and were confiscated by the troops.

"Bishop Retord with Father Charbonnier and Father Mathevon built themselves a little shelter deep in the forest and lived there for four months, kept alive by Christians who came by night with food. Their shoes had been worn to shreds by their incessant walking, and their feet were badly cut by the sharp pointed stones on the mountain sides, which the people call 'cats' ears.' Bears and tigers roamed through these forests. There was no good drinking water. One day in August when we sent a teacher with a message for the Bishop, his way was blocked by a magnificent royal tiger. The teacher got away safely in a way that seems miraculous. That very day the tiger had already killed and eaten two little girls who were pasturing their bullocks by the roadside.

"You may want to know if Bishop Retord is still in this forest home. His body is there, yes; but his spirit has gone on to a better world. His health was run down by this hard life, and he died October 22nd of a fever which found little resistance in his weakened frame.

"Thus ended twenty-five years of hard work and suffering in these missions. He had been a Bishop for fifteen years. He did not live to see the dawn of peace in this unhappy land. His life here was the actual unfolding of a childhood dream when our Blessed Mother appeared to him and carried him to the foot of a great Cross on top of a mountain and told him that his own life would be one crucifixion after another to the very end.

"All missioners have to follow the way of the Cross. Bishop Retord did so much more than the rest of us. His death in this terrible forest, where he was surrounded by cruel beasts and pursued by even crueller men and deprived of even the most common necessities of life, was indeed the death of the Cross, where he died stripped and beaten, like his Master.

"Some time after the Bishop died, Father Theurel, Father Titaud and myself had to run back to the mountains. We, too, knew what it means to walk over these terrible 'cats' ears' which tore the skin from our feet.

"We had two weeks of perfect peace in the depths of the woods. Each day we added some improvement to our Robinson Crusoe life. We collected rain water for drinking and for our cooking. We cut a little avenue through the trees where we could walk and say our Breviary. People from the village of Dong Chiem brought us provisions every morning. We even began a little truck garden.

"One morning six strangers appeared all armed. They said they were hunting tigers. We welcomed them, brought them into our hut, and then under pretense of going into the forest for more firewood, we excused ourselves. Once out of sight, we fled down the mountain to the place where we kept a boat hidden for emergencies. As we suspected, our 'hunters' were actually a patrol that had been sent out in search of us.

"From then on we felt it would be safer to live in our little boat, going from place to place. A young Christian brought us food every day, when he left his village 'to go fishing.' This amphibian life continued for some weeks until we were found out again. So we separated. I went back to my old district and lived for a while in the home of one of our teachers. Then I hid in a convent. I am still here. Father Saiget escaped from his prison and is with me here. There is a secret cavern beneath the house where we can hide if things get hot. Just now there is a lull in the storm. We have two of our teachers here, too, and we spend our time studying Chinese. The Sisters have moved to another part of the compound. There are sixteen of them, living in continual terror and they take turns watching day and night. They are delighted, however, with this opportunity of daily Mass and the Sacraments.

"We expect peace. A French squadron reached Touranne on September 1st. Three thousand soldiers are camped on the shore. Their arrival brought joyful hope to Christians and pagans alike, for the pagans hate this regime and attribute all the troubles of recent years, taxes and squeeze, crop failure and floods, to the wrongdoing of the Emperor and his subalterns. 'The cruelties against the Christians have brought down the vengeance of the gods on this dynasty,' they say, 'the Europeans are coming to save them, and this is only just.'

"A comet has appeared. According to their superstitions, this is a sign of war. This adds to the popular belief that the present government will soon fall apart. A rebellion is in the making. Once some encouraging word is spread about the success of the French force, the revolutionists will rise up all over the country. It seems strange that while the French squadron has been already three months in these waters, we have heard of no action."

CHAPTER NINE

Underground

*"In that hour, when night is calmest, sang he from
the Hebrew Psalmist
In a voice so sweet and clear, that I could not
choose but hear.
And the voice of his devotion filled my soul with
strange emotion;
For its tones by turns were glad, sweetly solemn,
wildly sad."*
— *The Slave Singing at Midnight,*
H.W. LONGFELLOW

"I am writing to you from a little dark hole, where the
only light I get comes through the crack of a door partly
ajar. It is just barely possible to trace these few lines. Now
and then I can read a few pages of a book. I have to be
always on the watch. If a dog barks, or if a stranger passes
by, the door is closed, and I get ready to disappear down
below where I have a hole dug out that is big enough to
hide me.

"For three months this has been my life. Sometimes I am
alone, sometimes my old friend Bishop Theurel is with
me, who was recently made Bishop to assist Bishop Jeantet.

"The convent where we had been hiding was destroyed
when the pagans got wind of our presence there. The
mayor himself came with a band of soldiers and surrounded the place. We disappeared between two walls and
watched through the cracks. We could see the soldiers
garrotting five or six of the older nuns who had failed to
escape when the others got away. They beat these poor

Sisters with clubs. They stripped the houses of every bit
of furniture and kept demanding money, threatening to
kill and burn unless they were paid what they asked. This
went on for four hours. They came so near us we could
have reached out and touched them. We hardly dared
even to breathe.

"They did not leave until the village elders invited them
to a banquet and drinking bout. Even then they left guards
around the place. At dawn the next morning we stole away
and hid in a compost heap in the yard of an old Catholic
widow."

This letter, dated May 10th 1860, was written to an old
college friend back in France, Father Paziot. Father Venard
told him of Bishop Retord's death. Bishop Jeantet,
then seventy years old, succeeded him and chose Father
Theurel as his Coadjutor Bishop. He was consecrated at
once, though only twenty-nine years of age. Theophane
gave his friend a description of the persecution raging at
that time, or as he said, he 'would paint a picture of it
for him,' because the only writing materials available were
a scrap of old paper and a brush such as the orientals
used to draw their characters.

"How would you like to be with us, dear old friend?
Here we are, three of us—one Bishop and two priests, ly-
ing side by side, day and night, in a space about two
yards square. The only light we have comes through three
little holes, each the size of your little finger. These are
punched through the mud wall. Outside, these holes are
concealed by brushwood thrown against the wall.

"Down below us there is a brick cellar, very cleverly constructed by one of our teachers. In the cellar are three
bamboo tubes which pass outside to the borders of a little
lake. On these tubes we will have to depend for our sup-

ply of fresh air if we are forced to hide in the cellar. In the village the same teacher has built two more hiding places of the same style with adjoining secret passages cleverly constructed with false walls."

Word was brought to the missioners in hiding of more people dying for their faith. Four more Annamese priests were put to death. One of the students, who came from one of the upper class families, denied his faith under torture, but afterwards was overwhelmed with remorse and came back to the mandarin of Nam Dinh to withdraw his denial and testify that he was still a Christian. He was thrown into the elephant pen and crushed to death under the animals' feet.

Most of the students showed astounding courage under torture. One of them, covered with blood, said to the soldiers: "Your pincers and clubs are nothing. Why don't you try something else!"

Admiral Rigault de Genouilly, commander of the French squadron, wanted to evacuate all the missioners to keep them out of danger until some sort of pressure could be brought to bear on the Emperor of Annam. The Admiral got word to Father Legrand de la Lyraie, one of the missioners in the eastern coastal area, who in turn sent the invitation on to all the other missioners. Father Venard and his companions replied that such a long overland journey to the sea under the existing circumstances would be entirely out of the question. They would have to stay where they were, hoping and praying for the best.

Theophane's father died August 26th, 1859, at the age of sixty-four. Mélanie, Henry and Eusebius were with him. Mélanie held a portrait of her priest brother before her father's eyes: "Look, Father," she said, "Theophane is here with us, too. You must bless him along with the rest of us." The dying man responded faintly: "Ah, that dear boy. I wonder where he is?" He gave them his fatherly blessing and then passed away peacefully.

They sent Theophane an account of his father's last illness and death, but this letter did not reach him. He never knew on earth of his father's death. Thus there is no mention of it in the long letter which he wrote from his underground hiding places the following spring and summer.

"We stayed in the yard of the old widow for about three weeks," Father Venard continued in his letter to Father Paziot. "I'm afraid you might be scandalized at our unconcern and the very light and happy way we took things. The officials were looking for us. They knew we were in the neighborhood. The house had been surrounded a number of times. A fallen away Catholic led them to the very house and yard where we were concealed. They turned everything upside down, broke through the partitions, and spent a whole day poking for us. But God was watching over us.

"Perhaps you ask: 'How could you possibly live in a place like that, without light and air and exercise?' That's right: how could we? Really I don't know. To be shut up between two narrow walls under a roof that you can touch, with spiders and rats and toads for companions, compelled always to talk in a whisper, every day getting news about the torture and death of fellow priests, about missions destroyed, students exiled, and what is so much worse—to learn about someone who denied his faith when put to the torture. It needs a very special grace, I admit, to put up with all this and still live.

"How is our health? We are like stunted plants in a dark cellar, stretching our lanky unhealthy branches towards the light and air. Sometimes I put my head close to the door of our hideout to get a breath of better air. How I envy those who live in God's bright sunshine and can have all the fresh air they want.

"I just had a note from one of my confreres who says that he has not seen the sun for eighteen months. At the top of his letter, with the date, he has 'From the Land of the Moles.'

"I live on. The weak points about me are my nerves. I need a tonic, but we have nothing. We have barely enough wine to say Mass. An Annamese doctor made me some pills which seem to help. I left the cave a few days ago to go into a house nearby. It was embarrassing because the daylight made me giddy, and I staggered into the house like a drunk. I seemed to have lost the ability to walk again.

"We heard that the French squadron had attacked the forts at Saigon and destroyed them. A French garrison was left guarding one of the forts and the campaign continued until April 1860 when the French withdrew from the country altogether. This move has baffled everyone. We had hoped to be delivered from this terrible situation, but it is better for us to put our hope in God, and He will deliver us in His own good time.

"As might be expected, the withdrawal of the French forces was the signal to intensify the campaign against Catholics. Mandarins who were known to have shown any favor at all to our people were dismissed at once. Road blocks were set up outside all villages, and all passers-by were screened in the usual way, with the order to step on the cross. Horrible blasphemies were composed about 'Zato,' which is the Annamese word for Jesus. These atrocities are too revolting to describe.

"Two new functionaries have been appointed for each canton, one called 'The Shepherd of the Flock,' and the other 'The Village Strong Man.' Their chief job is to hunt down the *'Zato'* followers, or Christians. Then there is a new law: an entire village must be punished for the offense of one of its members. This means that if a priest, especially a foreigner, has been harbored by some villager and later apprehended, the whole village must be destroyed, half the inhabitants put to death, the other half scattered to the four winds. If the mayor is found guilty of helping the priest, he will be degraded and sent into exile. If he reports the priest and betrays him, he will receive a reward.

"At this moment there are about twelve hundred of our former students roaming around the country. They really have no place to go. It is dangerous for them and for their families to go home; they cannot get work of any kind; and yet if they keep wandering they will inevitably fall into the hands of informers.

"You can understand what a heartache it is for us. We are the shepherds, and yet we can do nothing for our sheep. We have to lie hidden while they roam about among the wolves.

"In this general upheaval, the wicked become more wicked, while the timid and the poor are all the more oppressed. The women suffer terribly. Some of them are frightened so that they almost lose their senses. Our Sisters have been very brave and calm in the face of all this.

"The leading Christians of all the villages have been thrown into prison. We had seventy Annamese priests in this district. Ten have already died for their faith. Seven others are still in prison. We estimate that there must be about one thousand of our people hiding in the mountains.

"This letter has been written by bits, here and there. I

began it while hiding in a village that is predominantly Christian. The mandarin tried everything possible to break them. He failed because they have all stood firm, and he does not dare kill the entire population.

"To vent his spite he set up a reign of horror. His gangs go out and kidnap young girls. The parents may ransom them at a great price. Men, women and children spend days and nights hidden in the rice fields, to escape his atrocities, preferring the mud and exposure to the brutal treatment they know they will get at the hands of this tyrant and his thugs.

"During one of their vandalistic raids on the village they stumbled upon one of our hiding places. It was empty, fortunately. But they made a great fuss about it, and the next morning they had a crew of wreckers go through every house with spades and mason's tools to search for us. God was with us as ever, and we escaped. Now I am living with pagans in another village. They know that we are outlawed and that it is a grave risk to give us shelter, and yet they are kind to us. They are hospitable by nature and would consider it wrong to turn away anyone looking for food and shelter. It is all in God's plan to choose them for our protectors, no doubt, that in this way they may come to know about Him.

"I am just about worn out with the thought of all that is happening. This was once such a beautiful mission. It was yielding a rich harvest of souls. I feel like Jeremias lamenting over the ruins of Jerusalem. Again, it is like Ezekiel's vision of the dry bones. Will life ever again be breathed into them? I would only tire you if I kept on with this tale of woe.

"In God I have put my complete trust. I know that he will keep intact my faith and my hope and my love and that by the merits of Our Lord and Savior I will share the recompense of His friends.

"In June 1859 I wrote to my father. I'm afraid the letter may never have reached him. Please send this one to him, and let him feel as if it is written for himself. Ask him to pray more than ever for his boy missioner. Poor father, he must be getting old now. I wish I had some news from him and the rest. For two years I have heard nothing. Here is a note for my sister.

"Dear Mélanie—I meant to have written a separate letter to you, as also to my brothers. Instead, this must do for you all. I have had no news of you since December 1858. I know you have written and perhaps before many months your letters will reach me. Good-bye! God bless you! May you grow in holiness day by day. Your own devoted Theophane. Pray for me."

The missioners were being hunted from place to place like wild beasts. One by one, they were caught. Father Titaud died January 29th, 1860, worn out by this unnatural life. Father Neron was betrayed and arrested. He had to undergo the torture of the knout, and then starved in prison for three months, and was finally beheaded.

Father Venard kept at his mission work despite the constant attempts on his life. He had striking success in the village of Ke Beo where, as he said, he had to engage in a hand-to-hand fight with the devil. He rid the place of a lot of superstitions. He extended his work to the villages of Kem Bang and But Son. He intended to go on to But Dong, which at that time was the safest place for the priests, but first he went back to finish some work at Ke Beo.

CHAPTER TEN

Journey's End

"What matters Death, if Freedom be not dead?
No flags are fair, if Freedom's flag be furled.
Who fights for Freedom, goes with joyful tread
To meet the fires of Hell against him hurled,
And has for captain Him whose thorn-wreathed head
Smiles from the Cross upon a conquered world. . ."
— *The Peacemaker,* JOYCE KILMER

Six small boats approached the village of Ke Beo on the morning of November 30th. It was about nine o'clock. It was flood time, and the boats moved through the village close to the houses. They went directly for a building on the edge of the settlement, and then separated, each boat taking a different position to cover all approaches to the house. There were about twenty men in the group.

One of the boats pulled up close to the house and the occupants jumped out, led by a man named Cai Do, a leader in one of the neighboring hamlets. This man had engineered the escape of Father Neron from the Custom House six years previously. He had changed his allegiance since then. Father Venard watched the manoeuvre from inside and he knew what to expect. He disappeared between the double walls. The leader of the gang stopped at the door and called: "Foreigner, come out!" The catechist, a man named Khang, was trying to conceal some of the priests's belongings when the boats drew near. He stepped out and tried to talk them out of their plan. The chief pushed him aside and told his assistants to garrote him, and then going inside went almost immediately to the place where Theophane was concealed, kicked through the false wall and seized the priest.

It was a successful raid, accomplished quickly and easily. The gang retired immediately, taking their two prisoners with them. When Cai Do reached his own home, he put Father Venard in a cage, had a cangue placed on the neck of the catechist and then ordered a banquet to celebrate the capture. Later, when he brought the prisoners to the prefectural headquarters, he reported that he had captured them outside the village of Ke Beo. He said this because he thus expected a larger reward and because he wanted to save the magistrate of Ke Beo, his own son-in-law, from the fine imposed on villages that sheltered priests. His trick failed. There were too many witnesses to testify that the prisoners had been taken inside the jurisdiction of Ke Beo. A heavy fine was imposed.

Theophane was able to write little notes and get them out to his people. Here is one:

"*December 3, 1860.* My Dearest People—God in His mercy permitted me to fall into the hands of evil men. I was taken November 30th, the Feast of St. Andrew, put in a cage and brought here to the prefectural headquarters. I will do my best to send you a few lines with the aid of this brush. Tomorrow, December 4th, I am to appear before the judge. God knows what the future holds. I am not afraid. God will be with me, and my Mother Mary will watch over me as always. I hope I shall be allowed writing materials. A kind pagan has made it possible for me this time to send you my love from prison.

"I suffer very little. The people engaged by the Assistant Prefect are very kind to me. They visit me continually. I tell them about the teachings of Christ, and many have told me they believe completely in our Creed, that the religion of Jesus Christ is the only one that makes sense, and if it were not for the King and his terrible edicts, they would be Christians right away.

"Well, here I am in the arena of Confessors of the Faith. God certainly chooses the poor and the weak of this world to confound the mighty. I am confident that my battle will be my victory, simply because I am not leaning on my own strength. I will win by the strength of Him Who has already overcome death and hell.

"I am thinking of you all, dear father, dear sister and brothers. If it be my lot to receive the grace of martyrdom, then I promise that you will be more than ever in my thoughts. Good-bye, adieu, till we all meet again in Heaven. My chains are on the way. I will soon be wearing them, and I will be a witness for the Faith. Once more, good-bye!"

Bishop Theurel was eventually able to get this note back to France. He also filled in the various details. He said that when the mandarin in charge of the prefecture saw the prisoners, he was displeased with the whole affair. He protested that they should never have been arrested. The odium would fall on those who perpetrated the arrest. He saw no reason for taking them and he would let them go if he were not held to deliver such prisoners to the capital. He was attentive to the needs of Father Venard, had him transferred from the small bamboo cage to a large roomy cell. He had a lighter chain made for him and even invited him to dine at his headquarters. A detachment of soldiers escorted Father Venard and the catechist Khang to the capital. In his cell he wrote several letters which were successfully smuggled through the guards to Bishop

Theurel who later sent them on to France. Here is one to his family:

"*January 2, 1861.* My dearest Father, Sister and Brothers— I am writing to you at the beginning of this year which I expect to be my last on earth. I hope you got the little note I wrote telling about how I was seized on St. Andrew's Day. It is all God's will, so I hold no grudge against the traitor who betrayed me. I sent you a few lines from my first prison before I was put in chains. I wouldn't exchange my chains for their weight in gold; they are the bonds that keep me close to Jesus and Mary.

"The magistrate at the prefectural headquarters was kind to me. His brother came at least ten times, begging me to step on the Cross; I was too young to die, he said. When I was led off to the capital, I had to pass through an immense crowd of curious onlookers. A young Christian broke through the throng and knelt in front of my cage, asking for my blessing. Of course, he was arrested on the spot.

"Can't you imagine me riding along in my wooden cage? Eight soldiers carried it on their shoulders. When we reached Ke Cho, the ancient capital of Tong King, there was another big crowd. The remarks of the people, as we moved slowly through the streets, were interesting. 'What a handsome boy that foreigner is!' one of them said. 'You would think he is going off on a holiday, he is so happy looking!' 'He doesn't seem to be a bit afraid.' 'I can't believe he did anything wrong.' 'He came to our land to do good for us, and now they want to kill him!'

"We marched into the fort and I was brought immediately before the judge in the criminal court. My catechist Khang walked behind the cage; he still had that terrible yoke on his shoulders. I said a prayer to the Holy Spirit to give us strength and to speak through us, according to our Savior's promise. I asked Mary Queen of Martyrs to stay close and help us. The judge gave me a cup of tea and then got right down to business with the usual questions.

" 'Where do you come from?'

" 'I am from France.'

" 'Why did you come to Annam?'

" 'I came to preach the true religion to those who do not know of it.'

" 'How old are you?'

" 'Thirty-one.' Here the judge turned aside to one of his assistants and said: 'Poor youngster.' Then he continued:

" 'Who sent you here?'

" 'I was not sent by the King of France nor by his magistrates, but I came of my own accord. I came to explain the words of Jesus Christ to non-Christians, and my superiors in religion assigned me to Annam as the territory in which I should do this.'

" 'Do you know Bishop Lieow?' (The Annamese name for Bishop Retord).

" 'Yes, I know him.'

" 'Why did he encourage the rebel chieftains to recruit Christians?'

" 'Where did you get that information?'

" 'The Prefect of Nam Digne reported it.'

" 'I can testify that it is not true. The Bishop is too prudent a man to do anything so rash. Even if you have letters, I know they are false. I saw the instruction which the Bishop sent to his priests. He positively forbade them to join up with the rebels, and he said that he would a thousand times rather give up his life than in any way be instrumental in the shedding of blood.'

" 'And what about the military forces that took Touranne and Saigon? Who sent them? Why did they make war on our country?'

" 'I have heard some rumors of this fighting, but I have had absolutely no communication with these European troops, and so I cannot answer your question.'

"Just then the chief magistrate arrived and was hardly seated when he interrupted the judge's questions, shouting at me with a loud angry voice:

" 'You are the head of the Christian religion here. You look clever enough. Don't you know that the laws of Annam forbid Europeans from coming into our kingdom? What was the sense, then, in coming here to get killed? You are the one that stirred up the Europeans to make war on us, are you not? Tell the truth now, or I'll have you tortured!'

" 'Great Mandarin,' I replied, 'you are asking me two questions. First, why did I come here when I knew that foreigners were banned by law? I came because I am an ambassador of the Lord of Heaven to preach the true religion to those who will not scorn it, in no matter what kingdom or place on this earth. We respect the authority of Kings on this earth; we respect more the authority of the King of Heaven. Secondly, you say that I brought the foreign military forces to make war on Annam. I did not. Never in any way whatsoever have I wanted or incited war.'

" 'If that is so, will you tell them to get out of our country? If you do, you will be pardoned.'

" 'I have no power and no authority in such matters. If His Majesty the King of Annam sends me to them, I will ask the European forces to stop their war against Annam. If I fail in this mission, I will return here and accept the death penalty.'

" 'Are you not afraid to die?'

" 'Great Mandarin, I am not afraid to die. I have come here to preach the true religion. I am guilty of no crime deserving death. But if the people of Annam kill me, it will be my joy to shed my blood for them.'

" 'Have you any grudge against the man that betrayed you?'

" 'None at all. The religion of Christ forbids us from holding grudges, and teaches us to think well of and do well for those who hate us.'

" 'You are the head of the Christian religion here. You must give us the names of all the people and all the villages that have ever sheltered you.'

" 'Great Mandarin, they call you the father and mother of the people. Do you think it would be right for me to release information that would bring untold misery on so many persons?'

" 'Step on the Cross, then, and you will not be put to death.'

" 'I have preached the religion of the Cross every day of my life, and do you think I would go back on it now? I am not interested in what this life has to offer. I see nothing here worth buying at the price of denying my God.'

" 'If you are so fond of death, how come you always fled and hid when your life was threatened?'

" 'Great Mandarin, our religion forbids us to presume on our own strength. We are never allowed to throw our life away and we are expected to take all normal measures to preserve it. Since God permitted me to fall into your hands, I am confident that He will give me the strength I need to suffer any torture and to be faithful to Him unto death.' That was the end of my questioning for the time being.

"The officials then put my catechist through a similar examination. Afterwards they tortured him with the knout, inflicting ten strokes. He was brave through it all.

"My cage is near the door of the magistrate's headquarters. I am guarded by a detachment of soldiers. I have many visitors, a good part of them holding some office or other in the government. Some of them take me to be a doctor, others think I am an astronomer, or an astrologist, some sort of diviner or prophet. They think I know everything. Some of my visitors ask me to tell their fortune. They have a hundred and one questions about Europe, France, the whole wide world.

"I answer them as well as I can. You can't imagine their ignorance on some points, and you would surely laugh to hear their questions. I always try to link up their questions with something serious and get in a word or two about God, our Redemption, the next life, and so on. But they are a frivolous race, and have not much time for anything serious. They throw up their hands when I try to tell them something about philosophy or religion. Still, all in all, they are kind-hearted and they try to be pleasant with me.

"My soldier guards seem to like me. They are friendly and though they have been reprimanded two or three times for letting me get out, they still open my cage from time to time, and let me take a little walk. At times their talk is far from edifying. I try to show them that they are hurting themselves, that no one could possibly have any respect for them if they make a habit of such loose talk. They are more careful now about what they say. If they forget themselves and let slip some indecent word, they beg my pardon. Many are kind to me, but others are mean, insulting in their manner towards me, and their language is rough. May God forgive them.

"I am waiting patiently for the day when I complete my offering to God. It will mean actually giving my life, but I don't mind leaving this world. My thoughts are above and beyond it all. I feel that my sojourn here is just about at an end. I am getting nearer and nearer to our real homeland. Earth is slipping away, and Heaven is drawing near. I am going to God. Good-bye, dear father, sister, brothers. Please don't grieve over me. Live the years that are left to you on earth in unity and love. Be faithful to your religion, keep away from all sin, and we shall all meet happily some day in Heaven. Good-bye. I should like to write to each one separately, but I cannot. You know my heart. It is three long weary years since I have heard from you. I know not who is taken or who is left. Good-bye. May God have you always in His holy keeping."

Bishop Theurel kept in touch with Father Venard through the Captain of the Guard, a Christian named Huong Moi, who had sheltered missioners in his home and who worked himself into this post so as to be able to help the prisoner. The Bishop got word to Theophane regularly and in turn, he took charge of the letters written from the jail that were destined for the family back in France. The sentence had already been pronounced, death by beheading, but the date was not yet fixed. "Meanwhile," the Bishop said, "though in chains and locked in jail, Theophane is happy as a lark."

One day, among the visitors to the jail was a man named Tu who had been responsible for the arrest of four priests in 1859. He asked about Bishop Theurel. Theophane upbraided him for his hateful undertakings and told him that he was engaged in a vile trade and that his diploma as mandarin of the ninth class had been bought with treachery and blood and would surely fade away as a wild flower in the spring. The magistrate, the judge and the soldiers who were listening to all this thought that it fitted the man exactly. They laughed and applauded.

On January 3rd he wrote again to Bishop Theurel:

"A thousand thanks for your letter. The Great Mandarin is absent, so I think I can get this letter through safely to you. He used to allow a certain amount for my food. He has stopped this. I would have gone without anything tonight if it had not been for a man named Mai, one of the leading men here, who is also in prison. He sent me a bowl of rice.

"The new chief justice came to see me yesterday and asked all sorts of questions. He remarked that the happiness of the next world is doubtful, whereas present joys are certain. I told him that I could find nothing on earth that gives real happiness. Riches and pleasures do not satisfy very long; on the contrary, they bring along their own evils. I told him that my heart was too big for this world and nothing here could satisfy it.

"He was quite polite throughout our talk. He said that he had given orders to have me well treated. I told him then that I had nothing to eat that day, but he pretended not to understand. In spite of what he says, he has doubled my guard and is constantly sending someone to check on my cage to make sure that it is kept closed.

"The captain of the guard will try again tomorrow to correct the food problem. There is another good fellow among the jailers. His name is Tien. He is full of respect. He and the captain are not afraid to address me as 'Bam Lay,' a term of reverence used only for mandarins and persons of high position. The two of them were responsible for a little New Year's party—a cup of first-class tea.

"I wrote a long letter to my family on very bad paper which I hope you received. Just think: I am actually catching up with that line in our Departure Hymn where it says 'perhaps some day all the blood in my veins,' and so on. I can say. '*Very soon,* all my blood will be shed for Thee,' and 'My feet *are now* loaded with chains. . . .'

"Here in my cage there is abundant time for thinking, and I think about eternity. Time is, after all, so short. You still have work to do, and so you may say with Saint Martin, 'Lord, if I am still needful to Thy people, I will not refuse to labor.' But I can use the words of Saint Paul, 'I go now. The time of my dissolution is at hand. For you to live is Christ; for me to die is gain.' We always sang these words on All Souls' Day and All Saints' Day.

"For all I know this may be my last letter to you. I should have been very hapy to have gone on working with you. I love this Tong King mission. Now, instead of work, I can give my blood. I'm very happy. The people here at the mandarin's headquarters just cannot understand how I can keep singing. This is the one they hear most:

" 'O Mother dear, place me soon in our true home near thee.
   Noble Tong King, land blessed by God, thou glorious land of heroes of our faith,
   I came to serve thee. I gladly die for thee.
   So be it, O Lord. Amen.'

"O My Jesus, O Immaculate Mother, when my head falls beneath the axe, receive it as the bunch of ripe grapes in the vintage, as the full-blown rose which has been picked in your honor. Ave Maria! When I meet our Mother Mary in Paradise, I will say this also for you— Ave Maria!

"I should be very grateful if you could manage to send some little souvenirs to my family. My chalice was a parting gift from the family. Eusebius, I know, would be delighted to have it."

Since the officials had ceased to supply food for Father Venard, Bishop Theurel engaged an old Christian widow, named Yen, to bring him his meals. This was permitted. The arrangement helped also to get more notes back and forth. On January 6th Father Venard wrote again:

"Thanks for your New Year's wishes. And a Happy New Year to you, dear Bishop. The mandarin prefect's wife, a mere girl from Ke Cho, came to visit one day. She was so frightened she could not open her mouth. I hope you will be able to do something about the education of girls, if you ever have the chance. There is so much to be done to lift them from their present position as slaves and let them understand the beauty and the grandeur of Christian womanhood."

The captain of the guard arranged for one of the priests in town to visit Father Venard. There was another priest in the same jail, but the two had been kept apart. Father Tinh, one of the curates of Ke Cho, was brought in one day with the crowd of visitors. Theophane knew him, of course, but pretended that he did not. He asked the captain: 'Who is the gentleman that came in with you just now?' 'It is the *thay-ca*.' replied the captain. This expression may mean either priest or head of the family. It was the captain's own little joke, intended to let Theophane know that here was a priest, and letting the other people there believe that Father Tinh was just another curiosity-seeker.

The two priests were formally introduced as strangers and allowed to stroll in the garden. This gave Theophane a chance to go to confession, and receive the priest's blessing. After that, the whole group was entertained with tea, while Huong Moi, the captain, kept up his lively line of chatter to amuse the visitors. Father Tinh had the Blessed Sacrament with him, which he entrusted to the old widow Yen, and she in turn concealed it in some bread and brought it to Theophane in the evening. He enjoyed the presence of Our Lord till midnight when he received Communion. He referred to all this in a letter written to Bishop Jeantet, January 20th. The same day he wrote to his father:

"As my sentence is still delayed, I will send you one more word of farewell. This will probably be the last. The days pass quickly. Everyone here is kind to me. They all regret that the laws of the land condemn me to death. I have not been tortured like so many of the others. A slight stroke of the sabre will separate my head from my body, like the spring flower which the Master picks in His Garden. We are flowers which God plucks in His own good time. One is the blushing rose, another the virgin lily, and another the humble violet. Let's try to please Our Lord and Master with the gifts and fragrance He has given us. I wish you, dear father, a long happy and peaceful old age. May you carry your cross bravely with Our Lord Jesus to the Calvary of a happy death. You and I, father and son, will meet again in Heaven. Good-bye.

"From my Cage, in Tong King, January 20, 1861. My dear Sister—I hope my general letter to the family reached you. Now, as my last hour draws near, I want to send you a special word of love and farewell. Our hearts have been linked since childhood. Remember how you used to fix my box for me when I would be leaving home to go back to school, and remember the nice things you used to say to make the going away easier and cure my homesickness? Remember that night of February 26th, 1851, the last time we were together, my very last night at home? Remember we said we were like St. Benedict and his sister St. Scholastica, spending the whole night in holy conversation?

"Then, when I sailed across the seas and came to Annam, your letters were always my joy. It's only fair, don't you think, that in this last hour your brother should send you a final token of love and remembrance.

"It is midnight. About two feet from my cage there is a feeble little lamp that throws a flickering shadow on this piece of Chinese paper on which I am trying to trace these lines for you. Around my cage all I can see is an array of banners and long sabres. Off in a corner of the room some soldiers are playing cards. Another group is playing checkers. The sentries sound the hour of the night with their tom-toms.

"From day to day I am expecting my sentence. Who knows; perhaps tomorrow I will be led out to execution. It is a happy death, isn't it, that brings me to the gates of life everlasting. Most likely I shall be beheaded. You will cry when you read this, I know, Sister dear, but they should be tears of joy. Just think of your own brother—a martyr in Heaven! Only a few more short hours and I shall have left all this below to go to our true home. There, with God and His own chosen ones, I will see what the eyes of man cannot possibly imagine, hear beautiful harmonies beyond all our dreams, enter upon an unending happiness of which we have here only a very dim idea.

"But first the grain of wheat must be ground, and the bunch of grapes must be trodden in the wine press. May I be truly pure bread and wine worthy of the Master. I hope so, through the mercies of my Savior and with the help of

His Immaculate Mother. So, while I am still waging my battle I feel confident of victory. I leave you, my dear Sister, in the field of good works. Gather a big crop of faith, hope, charity, patience, gentleness, sweetness, perseverance which will be our wealth in the next life when we will be together again forevermore. Good-bye, Mélanie. Adieu! Your devoted brother.

"My dear Henry—I must send you these few lines of love and farewell. You were very young when I left home. At that time you knew very little of the world and its ways. I feel that you will not look for happiness where it cannot be found. The heart is too big to be satisfied with the sham pleasures that the world offers. You are now twenty-nine. Be a man. Don't waste your time on frivolities. Keep from evil, avoid occasions of evil, be faithful to your religion—all this means being a man. I am writing this to you at a very solemn moment of my life. In a few hours, or at the most in a few days, I shall be put to death for the faith of Our Lord Jesus Christ. I die convinced that you will always be faithful to God, and will love Him as you loved Him in your childhood. He is the God of your mother and father, the God of your brothers and sister. He is the God Whom the greatest minds of all time have served faithfully and adored. He is a God of mercy Who helps us to do right and to avoid evil and Who alone will reward us or punish us forever.

"Read these words often. They are from your very best friend, your own brother. Take good care of our father and our sister. Be a good son, a good brother, a good Christian always. Good-bye, dear Henry. Come and meet me in Heaven.

"Dear Eusebius—You would have good reason to be jealous if I failed to send you a few lines for yourself. You deserve them, too, for being so faithful with your long interesting letters. But it is a long time now since I last heard from you, and perhaps you are already a priest, and, who knows, a missioner? Anyway, by the time you receive this, your brother will be no longer in this wicked world; I will have already left for a better one where we will meet again some day. Your brother will have died a martyr!

"Remember—that was my boyhood dream. When I was only nine years old I used to take my pet goat to browse on the slopes of Bel Air, and I used to take along the life of Father Charles Cornay, and I used to tell myself: 'I'm going to Tong King some day, and I'm going to be a martyr, too.' God arranged a sort of magic thread to lead me through the labyrinth of this life, right here to the mission of Tong King and to martyrdom. Let's praise and thank Him together, dear Eusebius, for being so good to me.

"I love these people of Annam. If God had allowed me to live longer, I would gladly have given every moment for building up the Church here in Tong King. The people are good, so fervent and so loyal. My health has never been strong and I have not accomplished anything big, but my heart has always been in my work. But man proposes, and God disposes. Life and death are in His hand; let's live for Him and die for Him.

"But you are young and you still have many long years ahead of you in which you will guide your bark through the waves of this troublesome world. Put prudence at the helm and let humility be the rudder. God is your compass, and Mary is your anchor of hope. Disgust and bitterness may rise up and toss you about at times, like a howling sea, but you will always stay on top. Put your trust in God, and you will always ride the waves like Noah's ark.

"My little lamp here is burning out, and there is no light to continue this letter. Good-bye, Eusebius, until we meet again in Heaven."

On February 1st, Father Venard sent another note to Bishop Theurel. "The magistrate is astonished that my sentence has been so long delayed. The messenger boy from the palace has to pass my cage when he delivers the despatches of the King. Every time he appears, I ask him if he has my sentence, and the answer has always been 'No.' Every morning I feel that I will push off this day into eternity, and when evening comes I am still here. My heart tells me that death is near, and then I am bothered by feelings that the message, when it does come, will not be death. I fight these thoughts as tricks of the devil. The suspense is trying. Good-bye, dear Bishop. Will this be my last good-bye? Who knows? May God's will be done, not mine."

This farewell was the last. That night his sentence arrived, though nothing was said to him by the guards. About two o'clock in the morning he had his breakfast as usual and was allowed to walk in the garden. The widow Yen followed him, and when they were at a safe distance from the guard house, she said: "Father, today is the day; you are to be executed." Father Venard thought she must have picked up a rumor. He doubted it, because he had been told that he was to be taken to the King. The widow insisted: "It is certain. The elephants are ordered already. The soldiers know it, for they have been summoned. You have only a few moments before you will be taken away."

He hurried back to his cage. He gave the widow the few personal belongings he had as keepsakes to be passed around among his friends. At the same time, an old lady arrived, named Xin. She had the Blessed Sacrament with her. This was the fourth time that Father Tinh managed to send the Blessed Sacrament to Theophane.

The old lady saw that there was no time to lose, so she pushed through the crowd of soldiers, went to the cage and put in Father Venard's hands the tiny box containing the Host. Her boldness roused suspicion. The soldiers immediately rushed in, snatched away the box and brought it to their captain. Theophane called out to the old lady: "They have taken away my Viaticum!" He forgot everything in his alarm lest the Blessed Sacrament be profaned. The widow Yen went at once to the captain and told him what it was, that it was not, as he supposed, a poison to hasten death and anticipate the sentence. She explained that it was a Food for the passage from this life to the next. Besides, she added, if he should dare to touch It, he and his entire family would die forthwith. The captain gave the box to her, and since there was too much excitement to bring it to Father Venard, she handed it to the old lady who in turn took it back to Father Tinh.

The magistrate summoned Father Venard to hear his sentence. Theophane had been saving his best clothes for this day. It was in the usual native Indochinese style, a long robe of black silk over an inner garment of white cotton. He put it on and then went out to stand before the magistrates. When the death sentence was announced to him, he made a little speech. It was a formal declaration that he had come to Tong King only to teach the true religion, and that he was going to die for the same cause. He ended by saying to the judges: "One day we shall meet again, at the tribunal of God." The chief magistrate jumped up and shouted: "I will have no insolence!"

The escort started then for the execution grounds. Two hundred soldiers under a lieutenant colonel made up the guard. Two elephants were in the procession. As they passed through the town, Theophane sang psalms and hymns in Latin. An enormous crowd was waiting at the place of execution. The soldiers formed a big ring to keep the people back, but the old widow Yen, just as brave as ever, broke through the ring and was allowed to stay with the missioner to the end.

Father Venard looked over the crowd, hoping to see Father Tinh and get a last absolution and blessing. Father Tinh, however, did not know that the command had been given, and was not there. Theophane gave his sandals to the faithful old lady. The soldiers took off his chains. They hammered the nails out of the rings that were fastened around his neck and ankles. Then they pushed everyone, including the widow Yen, out of the circle.

The executioner was a hideous hunchback, named Tue. He had been a soldier; at that time he was the town buffoon. On March 25th of the previous year, he had decapitated four priests, and he asked for this opportunity as well that he might have the martyr's clothes.

He asked Father Venard, just as he might barter with an ordinary criminal, what he would give him to be executed promptly and well. "The longer it lasts the better it will be," replied Theophane. The hunchback saw that the missioner's clothes were new and clean. He would like to get them without blood stains. He asked Theophane to strip. The priest refused. 'You are to get *lang-tri*," the man lied. That meant that the feet, legs, hands, arms would be cut off at the joints and the trunk sawn into four parts.

Either because he believed the lie, or because he was willing to imitate the humiliation of Our Savior, or perhaps also to get rid of the importunities of this vile hunchback, Theophane took off all his clothes except his trousers.

His elbows were tied tightly behind his back, forcing him to hold his head up for the fatal stroke. He was fastened to a stake that was set loosely in the ground.

At a given signal, Father Venard received the first stroke of the sabre. It was simply a trial blow by the merciless executioner and did not enter the flesh deeply. The next stroke, more vigorous, cut the head nearly off; the stake gave way and fell with the priest to the ground. Then the executioner, finding his sword blunt, took another and hacked at the neck, while indignant murmurs rose from the crowd.

Then the hunchback seized the fallen head by the ear and held it up to the lieutenant colonel who presided at the execution. The officer instructed the local authorities to keep watch for three days during which the head was to be exposed publicly. With this done, he instantly ordered the troops to fall in and march back to their quarters.

The moment the troops were gone, the widow Yen and other women rushed to the spot and soaked handkerchiefs, towels and bits of paper in the martyr's blood. Every trace of it was claimed so that there could not be found afterwards even a blade of grass with a stain of blood on it.

A group of Christians, helped by a good pagan, claimed the body and buried it in a shallow grave where it could be readily disinterred. The head was placed in a box, by the magistrate's order, and put at the top of a pole. One of the Christians had an exact duplicate of the box made, hoping to substitute it for the one with Father Venard's head, but the place was too well guarded.

At the end of three days, a guard was supposed to throw the head into the river. He had been bribed by the Christians to fasten a fish hook in the ear with two hundred yards of line and a floater. This would make it possible to recover the head. In his excitement, he made a bad job of it, shook the line free of the head, which then sank and was lost for the moment. On February 15th some friendly pagans found the head and brought it to the Christians. The fish hook was still in the ear with about an inch of the line. It was brought to Bishop Theurel who identified it, clipped some of the hair to send to the family in France and returned the head to a sealed vase to be hidden in a Christian home until some future day when peace would return to the land and it might be buried together with the rest of the remains. The condition of the flesh around the ear showed how it had been hacked by the inhuman executioner.

Thus he died, just as he had hoped so many years before when, as a boy of nine years, he stood on the slopes of the Golden Valley, tending his goats, and told himself that he would go to Tong King some day and die for his God. It was a simple life, full of little things done in a beautifully big way, and he died as he had lived, full of childlike trust, in the love of Jesus, Mary and Joseph and of his dear ones at home.

Epilogue

"Out of the mouth of the Mother of God
Like a little word came I;
For I go gathering Christian men
From sunken paving and ford and fen,
To die in a battle, God knows when,
By God but I know why."
— *The Ballad of the White Horse,* G.K. CHESTERTON

When Theophane Venard fell in his own blood early on that morning of February 2nd 1861, the tyrants thought that they were killing off the Christian religion. Actually, they were watering the seed. In Vietnam today you see church towers rising from practically every one of the hundreds of pretty little villages which, with their heaped up bunches of foliage, break the monotony of the wide green carpet of rice fields. There is one Catholic in every ten persons; they total over a million and a half. The churches are crowded on Sunday, and there is a large gathering on weekdays, too. Vocations to the priesthood and to the religious life are numerous. There are several Carmelite convents and Cistercian monasteries. In June 1952, one hundred years after the ordination of Theophane Venard, ninety years after his death, the Church in that land had 1,500 native priests and 4,000 native Sisters.

In a beautiful ceremony at St. Peter's in Rome, June 2nd, 1909, Father Venard was declared Blessed. One detail of this ceremony sent a thrill of triumph through the assembly. A painting of the Martyr had been placed within the huge gold gloria of Bernini, over the main altar. It was hidden from view by a curtain which hung directly in front of the picture. When the papal documents had been read proclaiming the heroic virtues of Blessed Theophane Venard, the choir took up the *Te Deum*, the Church's triumphal chant of praise, and immediately the drape fell away leaving Blessed Theophane high above the altar of the Vatican basilica, appearing in glory before the throngs of pilgrims that had gathered in Rome for the occasion. In the afternoon of the same day, Pope Pius X went to St. Peter's in solemn procession to venerate the relics of the Martyr.

Father Venard was killed, but his spirit never died. Father John Baptist Hogan, who was ordained with Father Venard at Paris, was driven from France by Communists of the First International. He came to America, became superior of St. John's Seminary in Boston, and read to his students the letters we have seen in the foregoing chapters. Among those students was one, James Anthony Walsh, who told himself that American boys could be just as grateful for their faith as Blessed Theophane Venard was, and just as generous in bringing it to others.

Later, after ordination, Father James Anthony Walsh used his skill as a writer and speaker to promote the idea of an American seminary to train young men for the foreign mission priesthood. He discovered that Father Thomas Frederick Price, of North Carolina, had the same idea. These two priests were sent to Rome by the Archbishops and Bishops of the United States to seek the Holy Father's approval for such a seminary, and on the feast of Saints Peter and Paul, June 29, 1911, Pope Pius X authorized them to start the Catholic Foreign Mission Society of America.

In the fall of 1912, they opened their first seminary on Sunset Hill, near Ossining, New York, and called it "Maryknoll." The next year, in September, 1913, they started a preparatory college in Scranton, Pennsylvania, and three years later they acquired a more suitable tract of land at Clarks Summit in the Abington Hills, eight miles from Scranton. There the present college was built and called "The Venard" after its patron, Blessed Theophane Venard.

Hundreds of boys have gone through the Venard. Most of those who completed their training for the priesthood are hard at work bringing the blessings and the joys of our religion to the people of Asia, the Pacific, Africa, Hawaii, the Philippines, South and Central America. Some have died. Some of them have been killed—one garroted by Manchurian outlaws, one shot down by bandits on a last-minute mission trip before setting out for home on furlough. One fell from a truck in the mountains of Peru. One was carried off from his mission by an enemy patrol during World War II and never heard from again. One died after giving the best years of his life to lepers banished from their homes in South China. Others died before their time, their health broken by difficulties and the rigors of strange climes. Many of them have been in prison during the reign of Red terror in China. Their letters are full of experiences that vividly recall the last years of Theophane Venard, whose letters they had read as students only a few short years before.

The boy from the Golden Valley started something when he said he would sail across the seas and be a martyr. Many American boys have caught the idea and are following him. They have come from the sidewalks of New York and from the sunny hills of California, from the farms of Iowa and Wisconsin and from the towns of New England and Pennsylvania. From Canada to Mexico, from Washington to Texas, from Maine to Florida and from just about all the states in between, from high school, college and university, from the football fields of Notre Dame and Fordham, Marquette and a score of others, from the Army, the Navy, the Marines and the Air Force, they have come to Maryknoll and have gone back to the world as missioners.

"Humanity wants to be able to hope again," Pope Pius XII said. The world has lost its optimism because it has been disappointed over and over again. It is learning the hard way that real peace cannot be fashioned by poor weak man left to himself and working alone. Mankind can have real peace, just as soon as it learns where to turn. That peace is in the heart of every man filled with the point of view of Christ, who tries to think and speak and do as He taught. It is Heaven's gift to all men. It is intended for everyone in the human family. It is the gift that these boys from America's Golden Valleys have seen and have set themselves to bring to others by obeying the command, "Going teach all nations!"